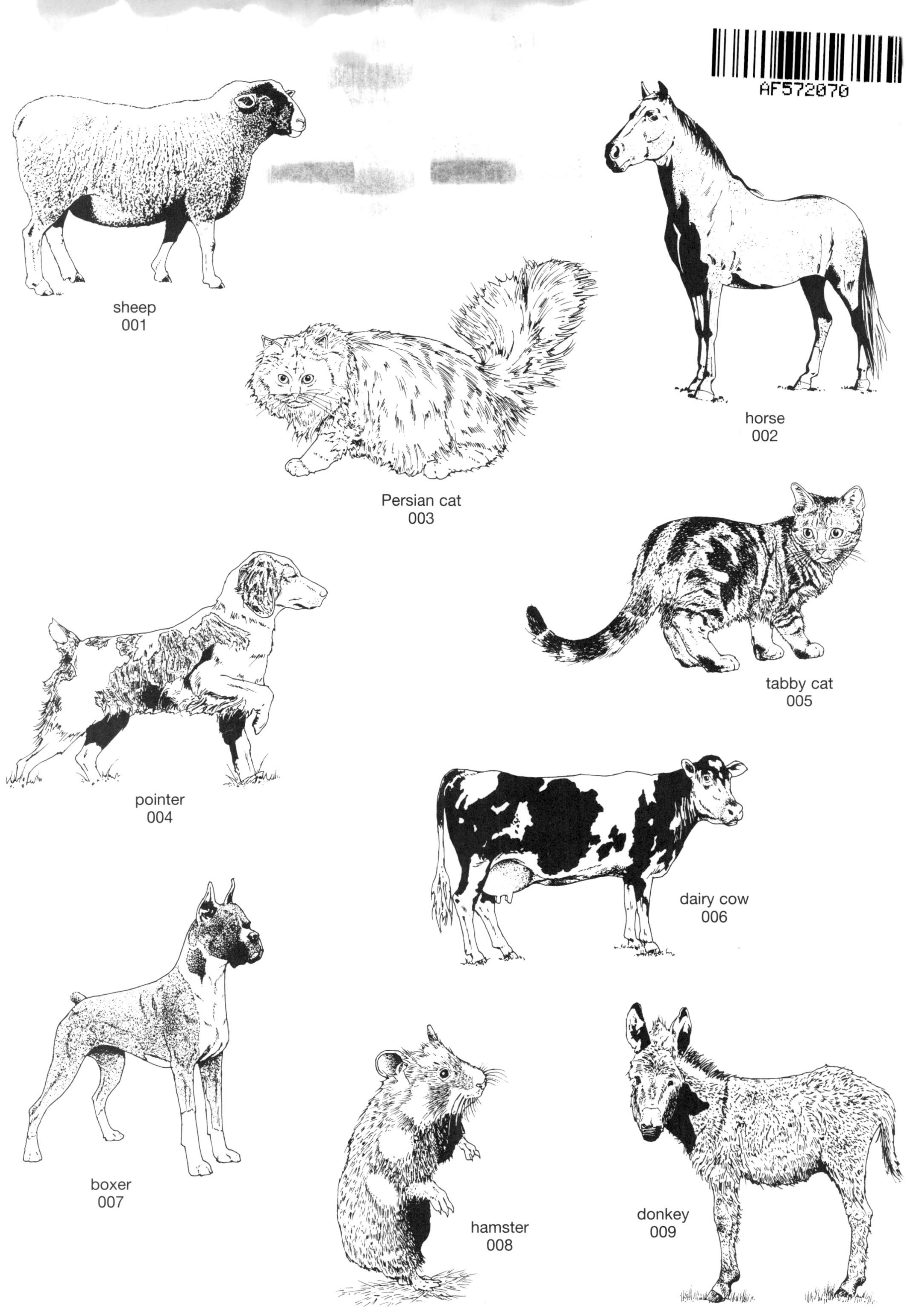

sheep
001

horse
002

Persian cat
003

pointer
004

tabby cat
005

dairy cow
006

boxer
007

hamster
008

donkey
009

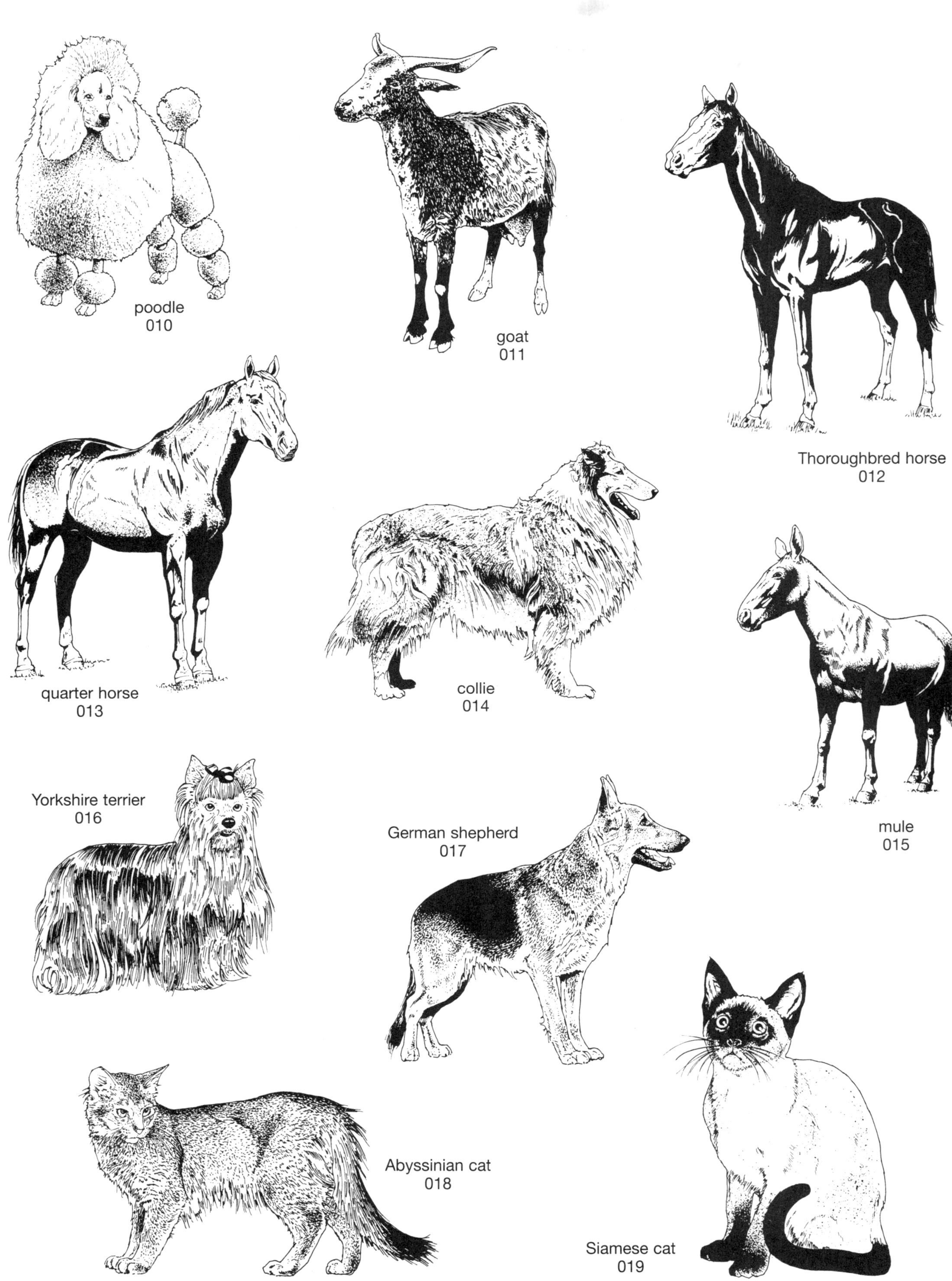
poodle
010
goat
011
Thoroughbred horse
012
quarter horse
013
collie
014
mule
015
Yorkshire terrier
016
German shepherd
017
Abyssinian cat
018
Siamese cat
019

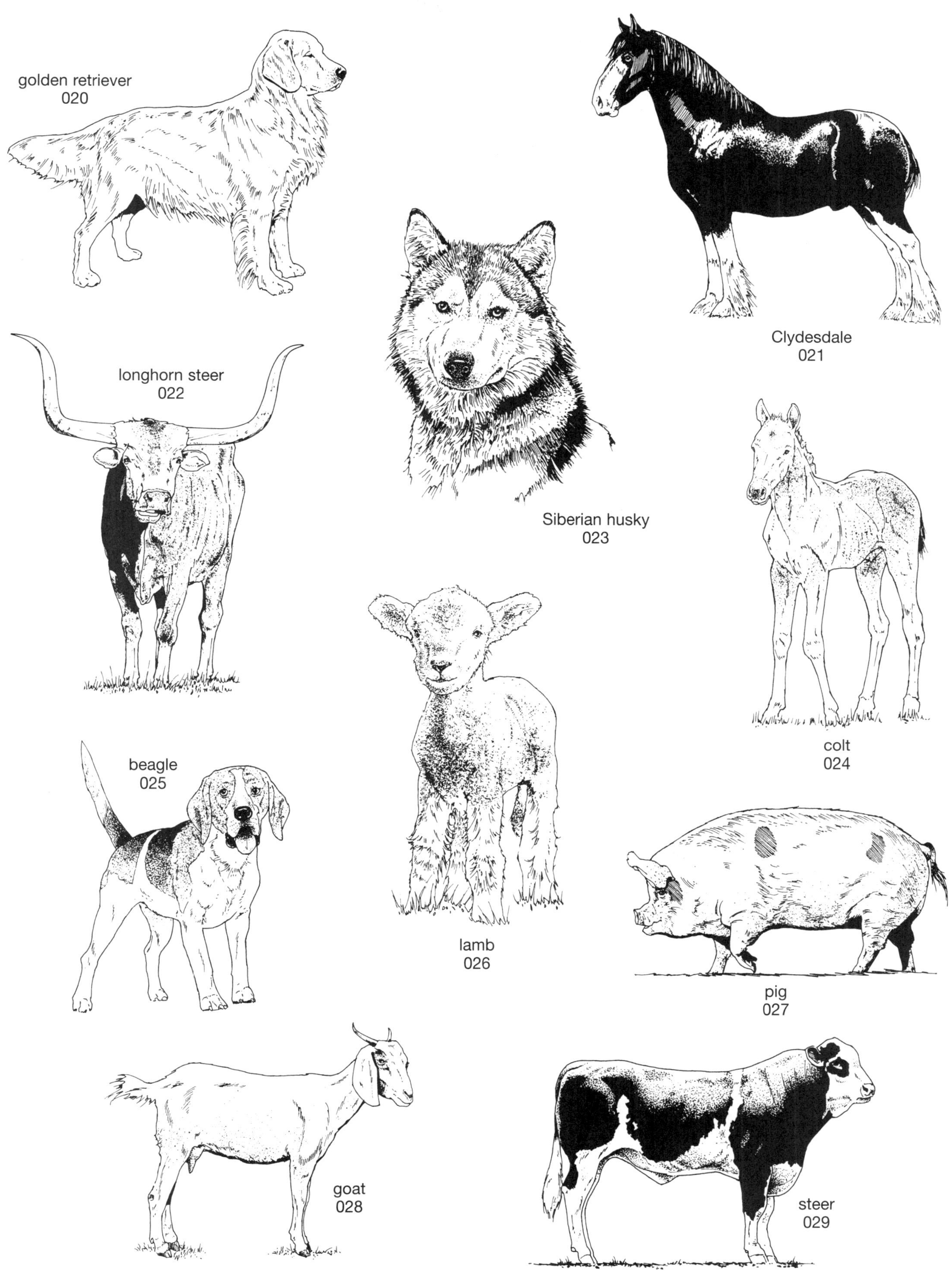
golden retriever
020
Clydesdale
021
longhorn steer
022
Siberian husky
023
colt
024
beagle
025
lamb
026
pig
027
goat
028
steer
029

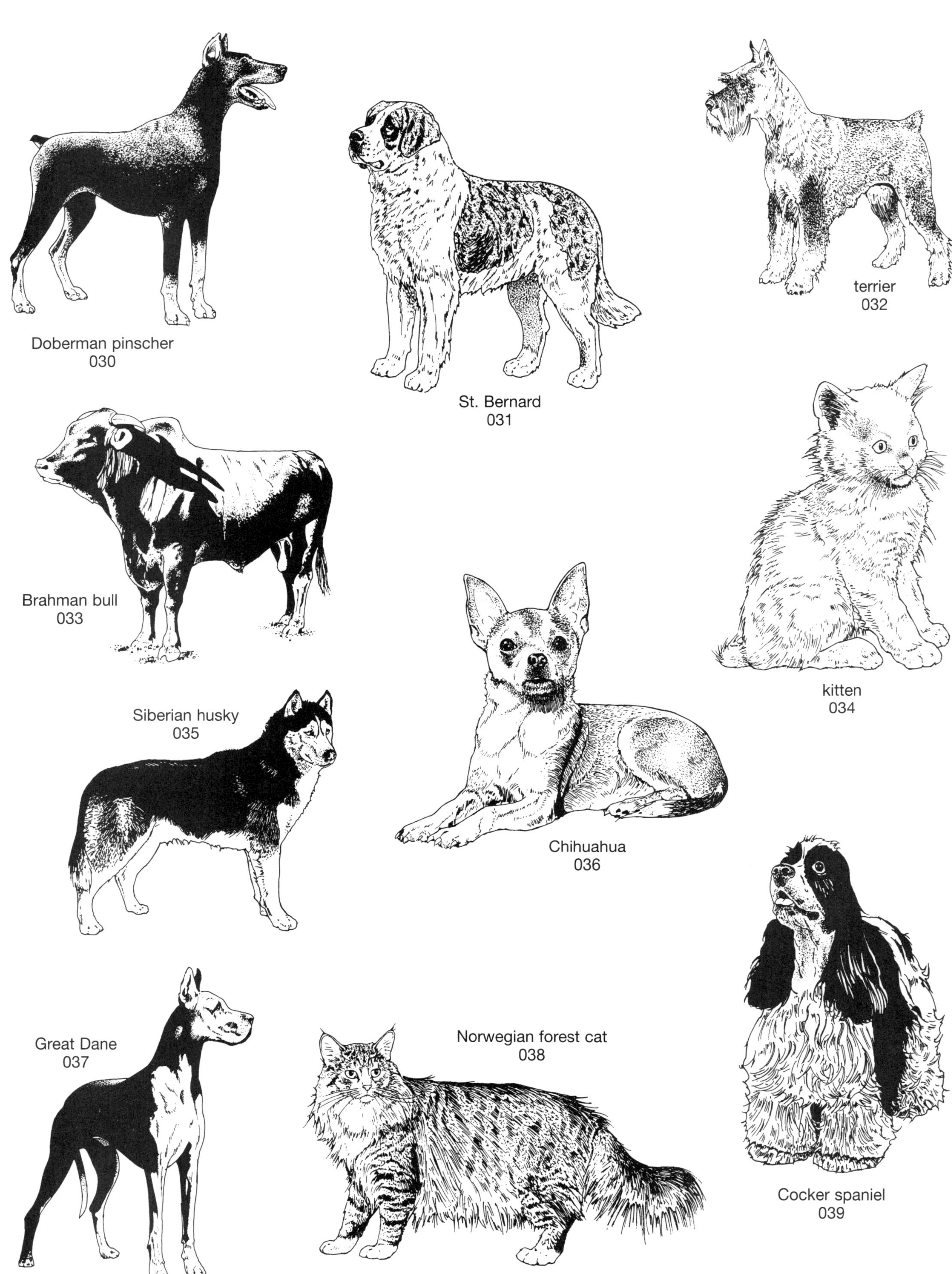

Doberman pinscher
030

St. Bernard
031

terrier
032

Brahman bull
033

kitten
034

Siberian husky
035

Chihuahua
036

Great Dane
037

Norwegian forest cat
038

Cocker spaniel
039

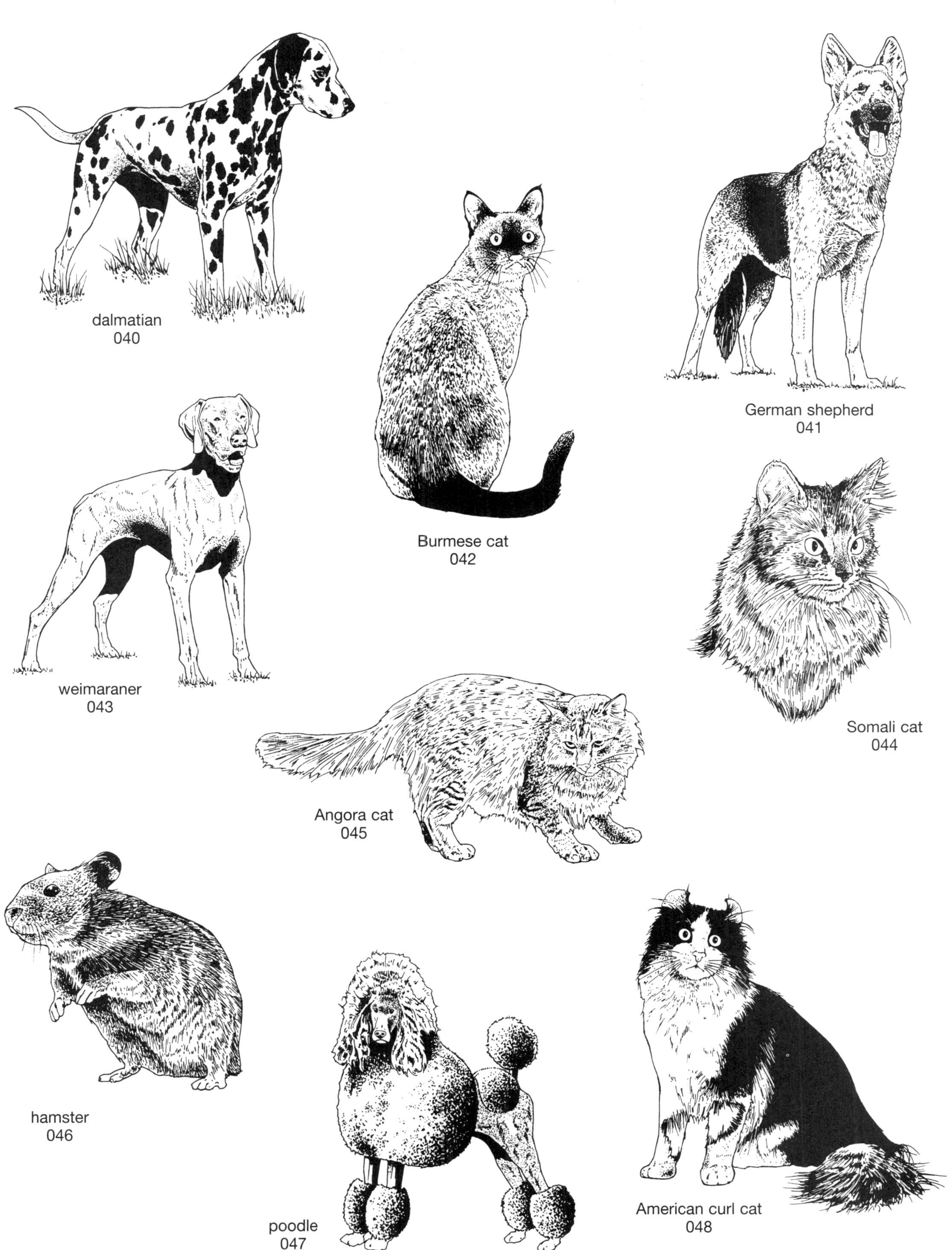

dalmatian
040

German shepherd
041

Burmese cat
042

weimaraner
043

Somali cat
044

Angora cat
045

hamster
046

poodle
047

American curl cat
048

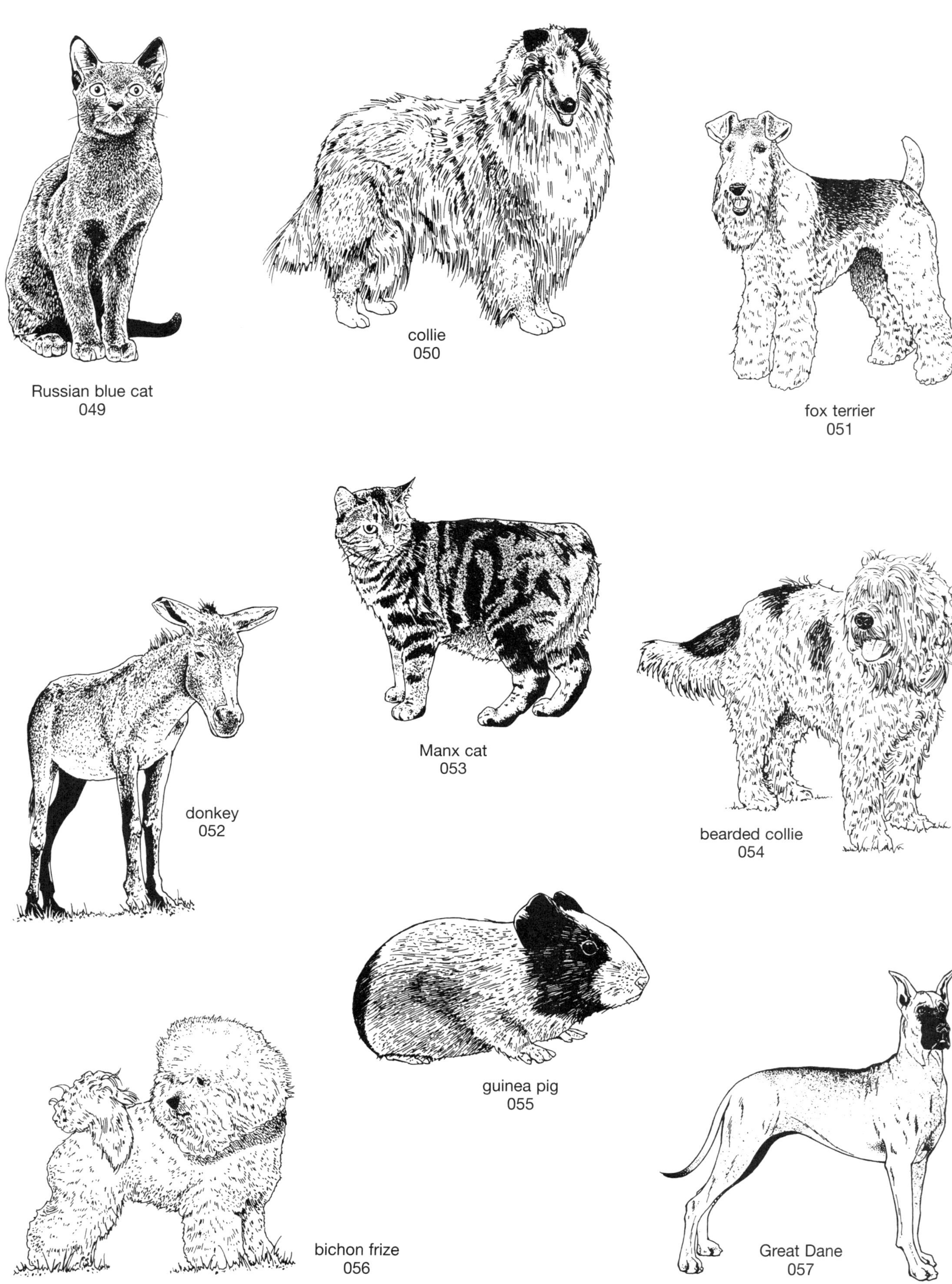

Russian blue cat
049

collie
050

fox terrier
051

donkey
052

Manx cat
053

bearded collie
054

guinea pig
055

bichon frize
056

Great Dane
057

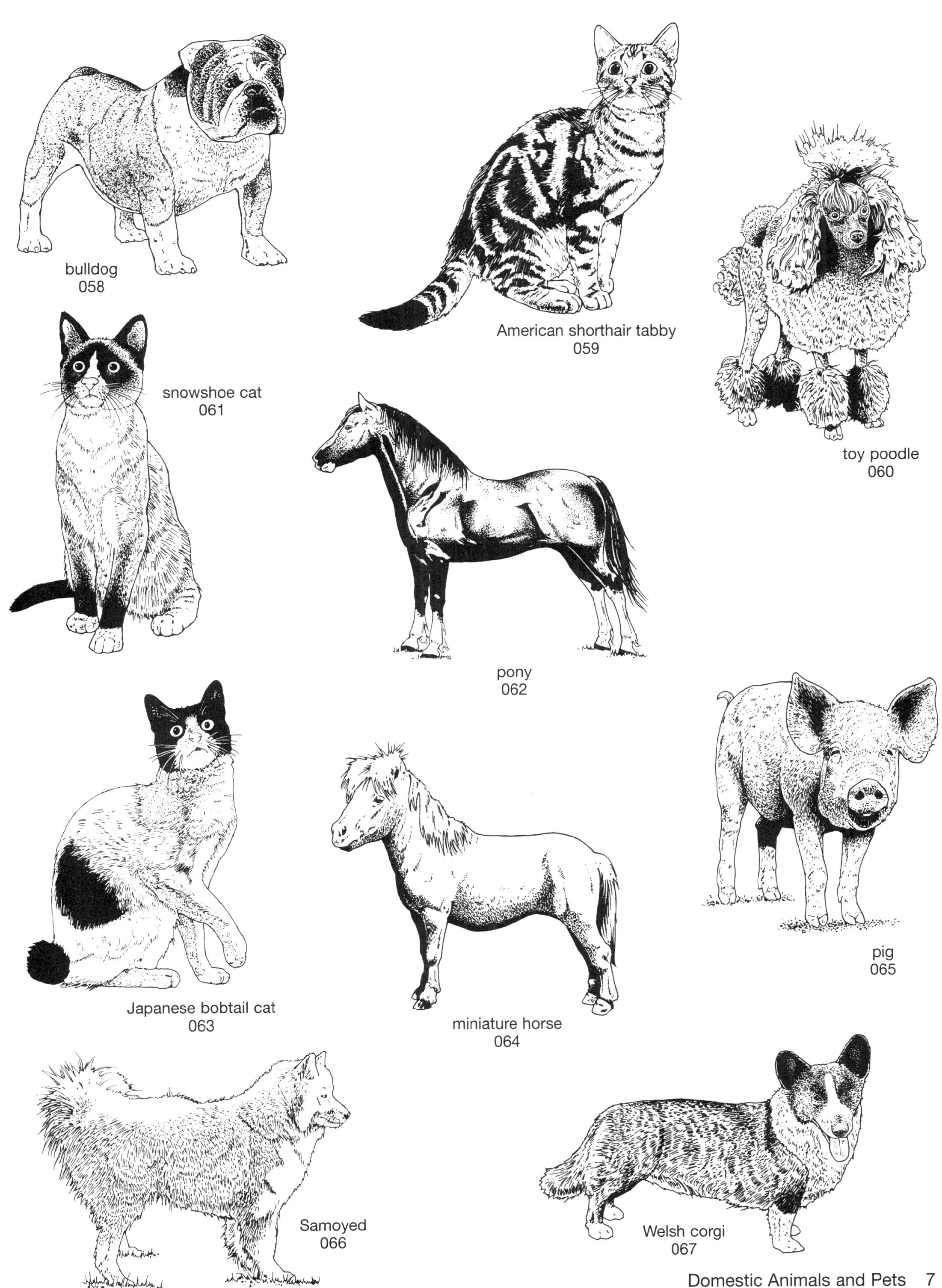
bulldog
058
American shorthair tabby
059
toy poodle
060
snowshoe cat
061
pony
062
Japanese bobtail cat
063
miniature horse
064
pig
065
Samoyed
066
Welsh corgi
067

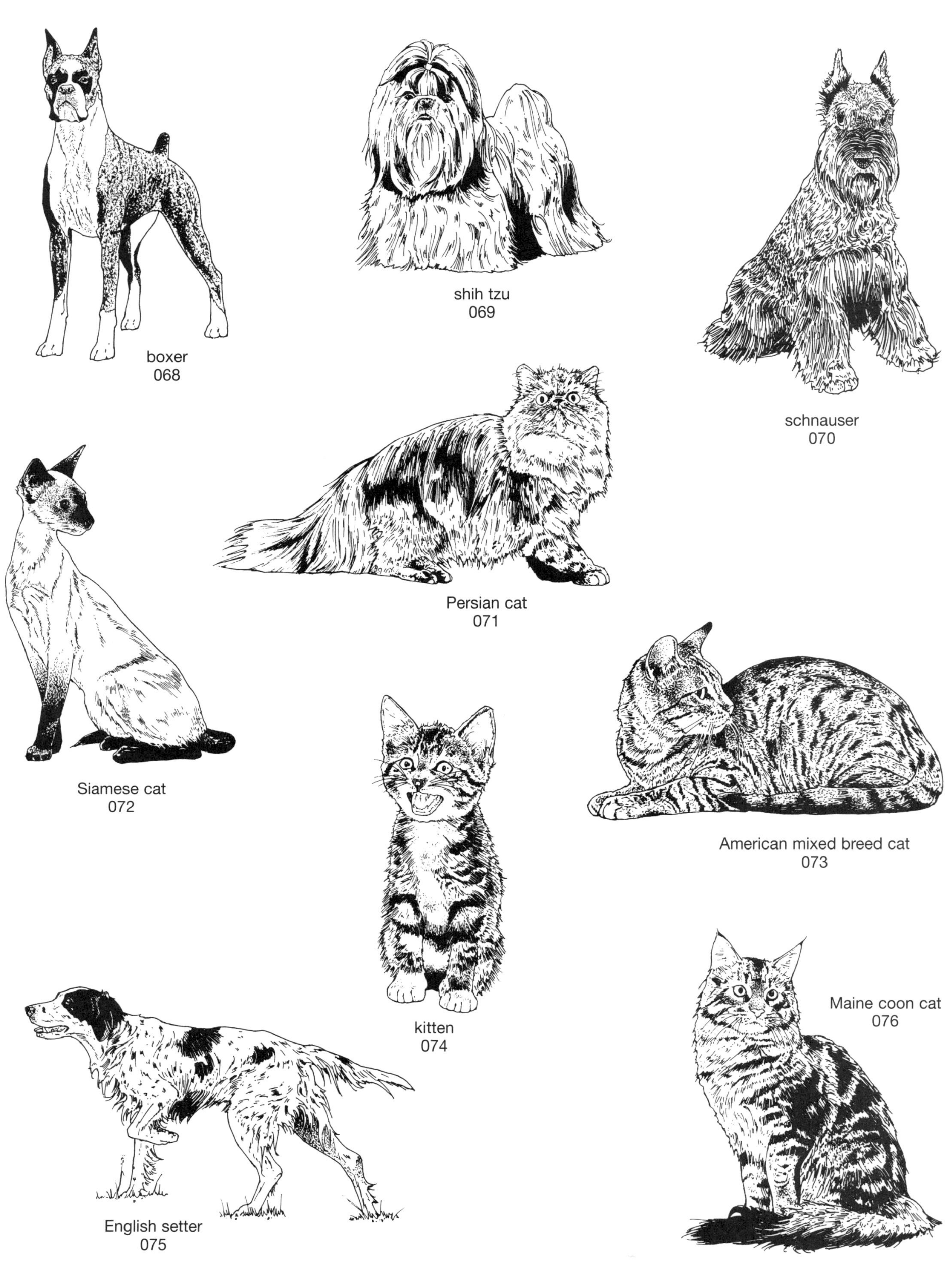

boxer
068

shih tzu
069

schnauser
070

Persian cat
071

Siamese cat
072

American mixed breed cat
073

kitten
074

English setter
075

Maine coon cat
076

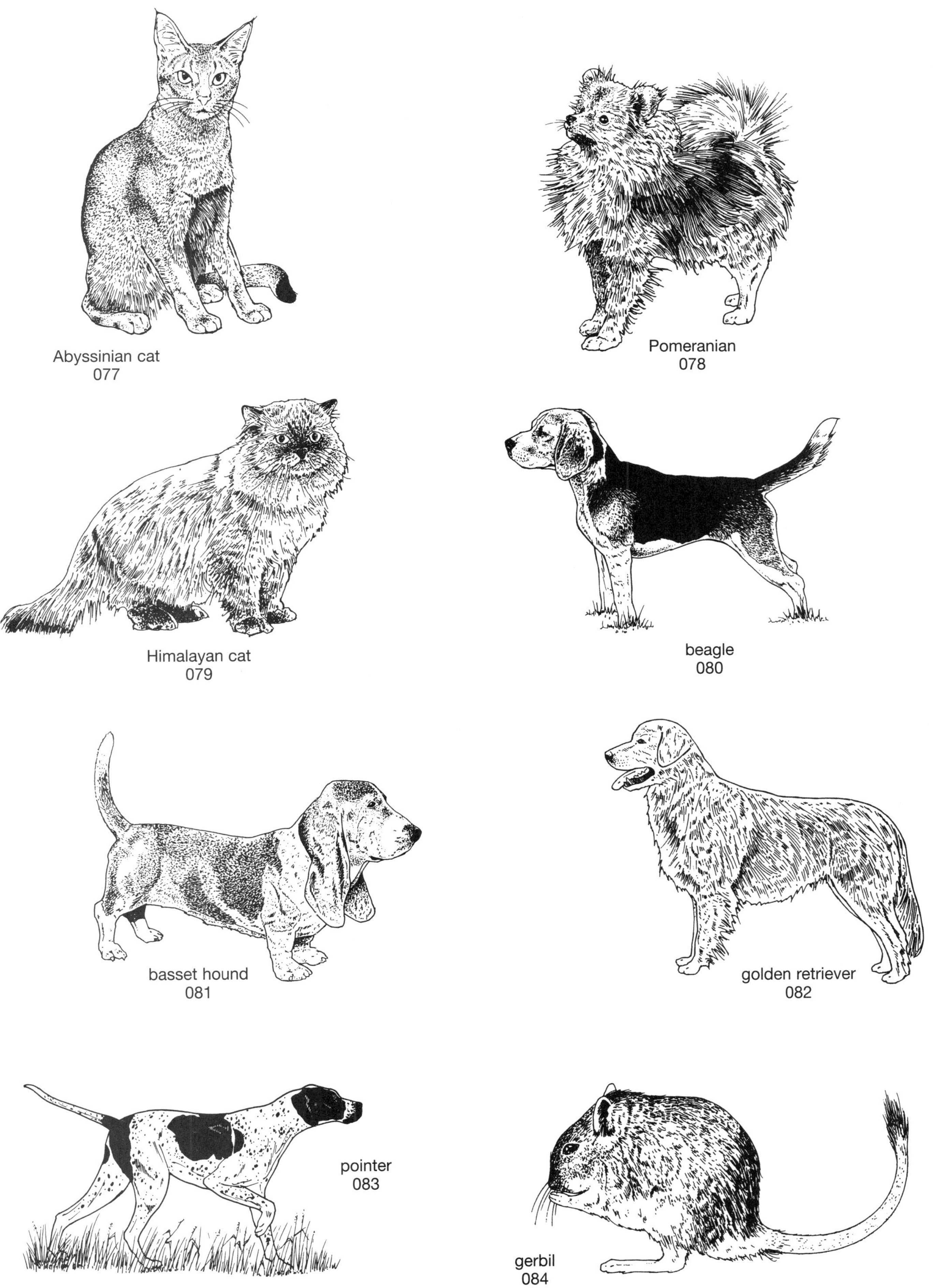
Abyssinian cat
077
Pomeranian
078
Himalayan cat
079
beagle
080
basset hound
081
golden retriever
082
pointer
083
gerbil
084

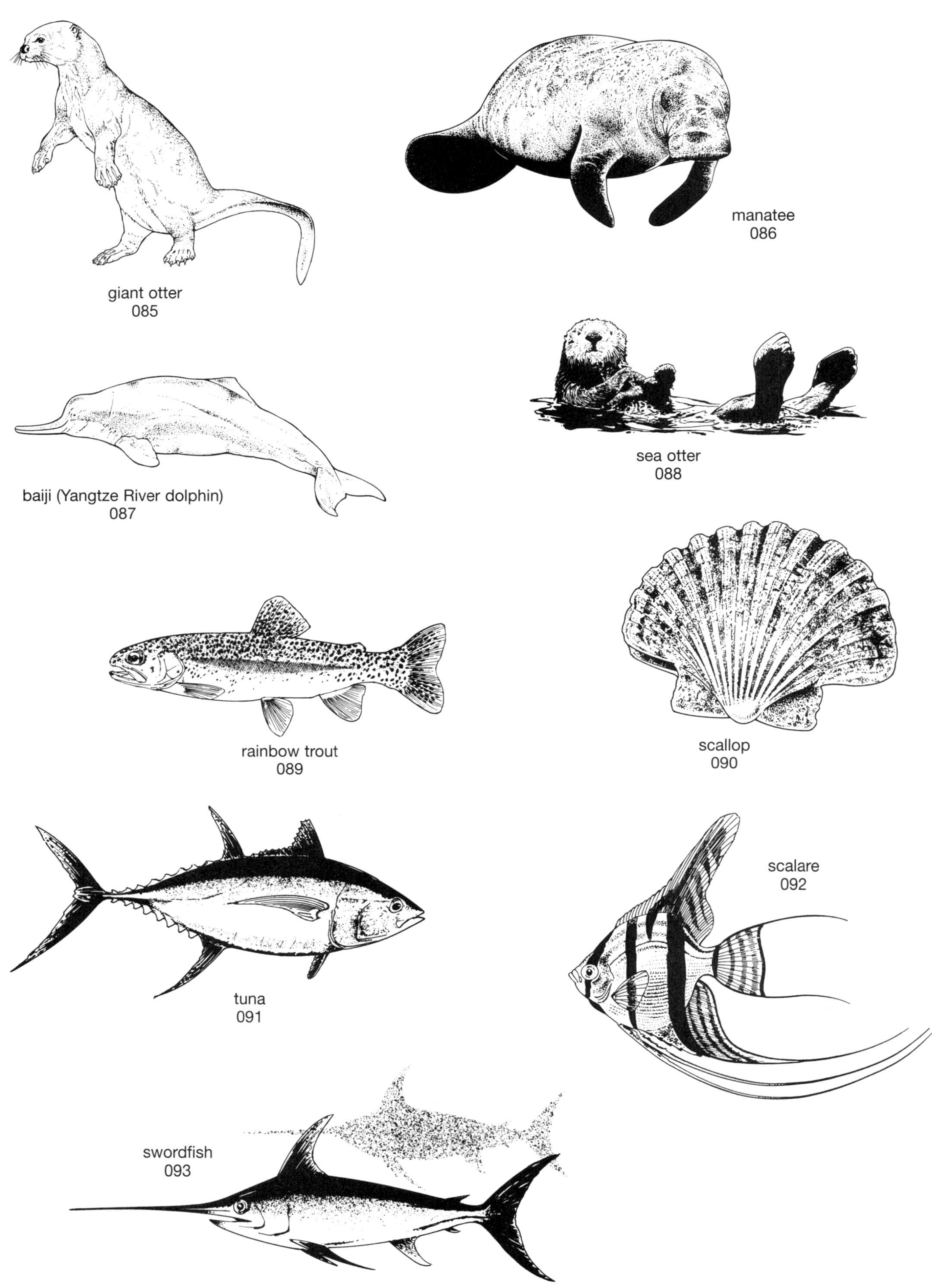
giant otter
085
manatee
086
sea otter
088
baiji (Yangtze River dolphin)
087
rainbow trout
089
scallop
090
scalare
092
tuna
091
swordfish
093

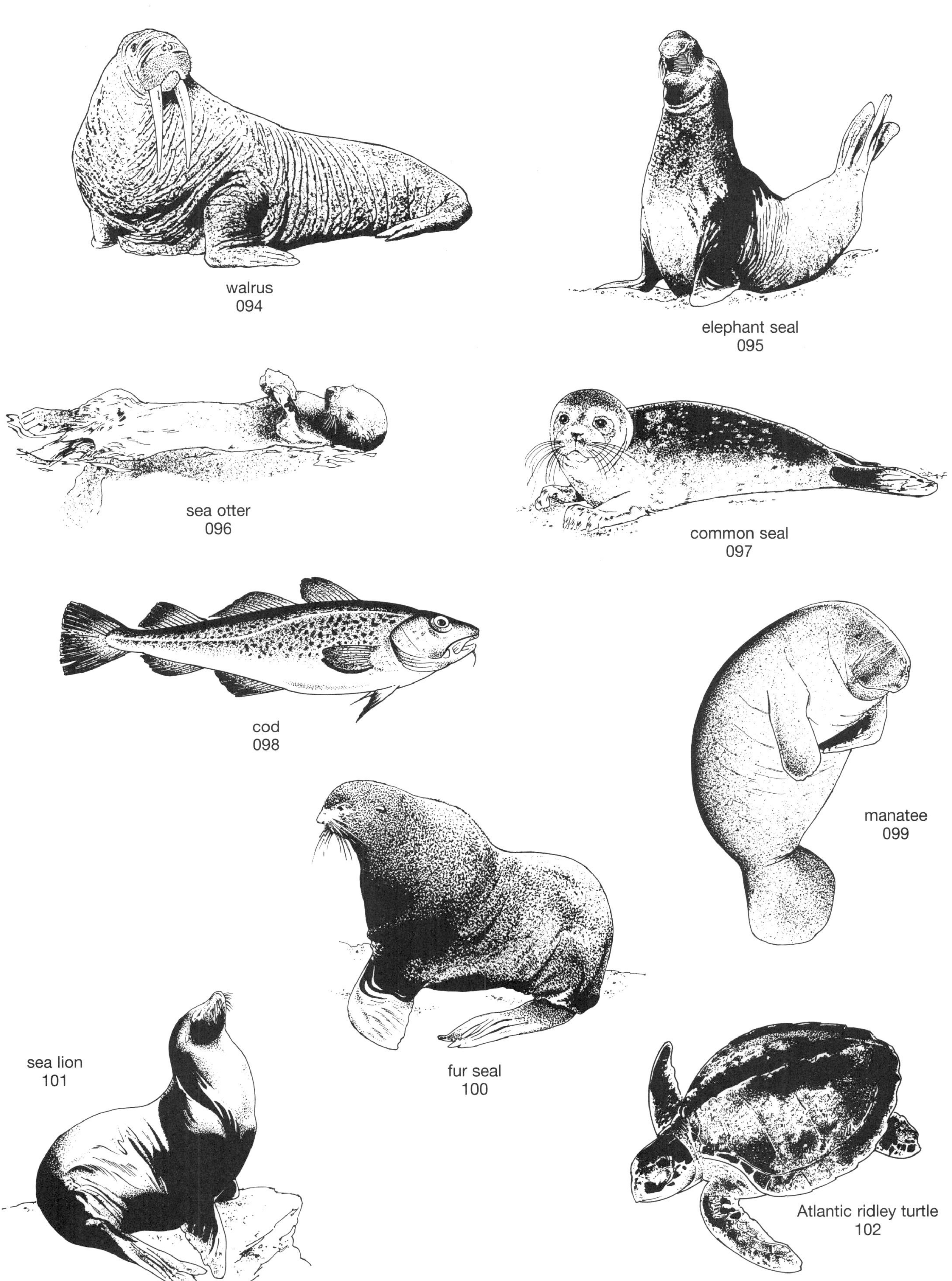
walrus
094
elephant seal
095
sea otter
096
common seal
097
cod
098
manatee
099
fur seal
100
sea lion
101
Atlantic ridley turtle
102

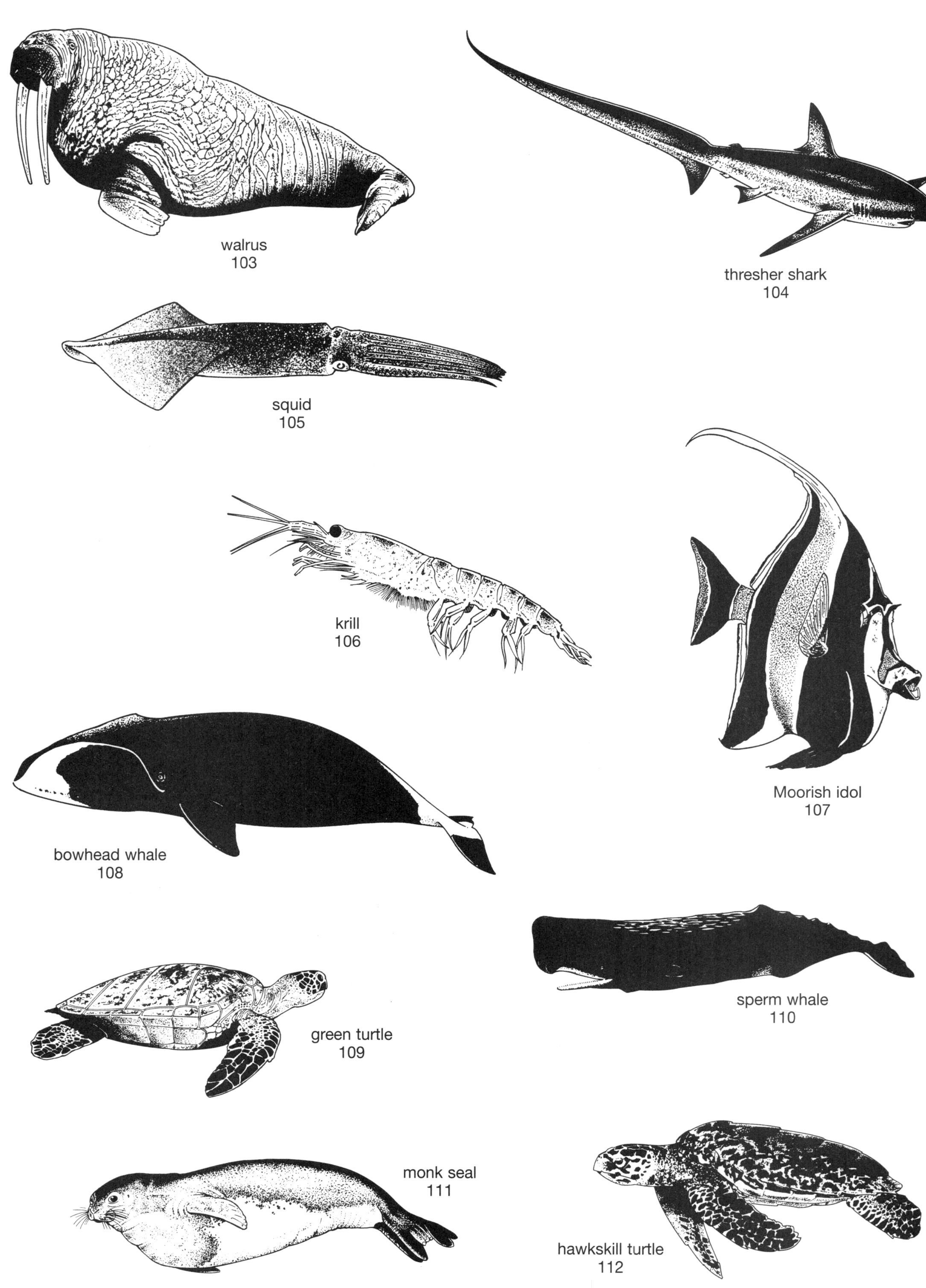
walrus
103
thresher shark
104
squid
105
krill
106
Moorish idol
107
bowhead whale
108
green turtle
109
sperm whale
110
monk seal
111
hawkskill turtle
112

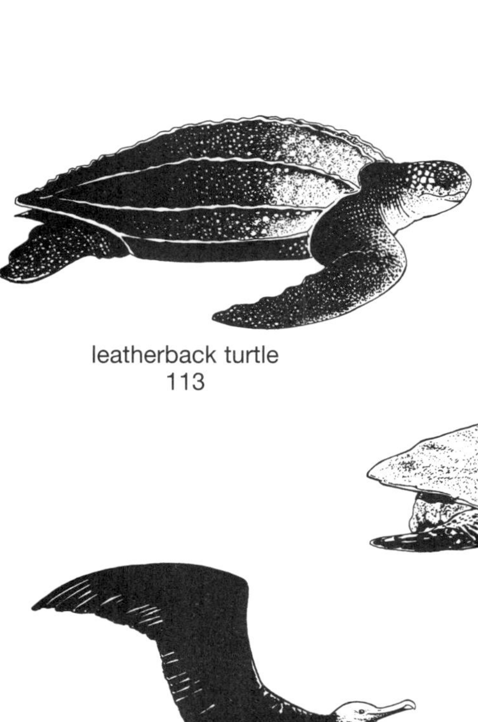

leatherback turtle
113

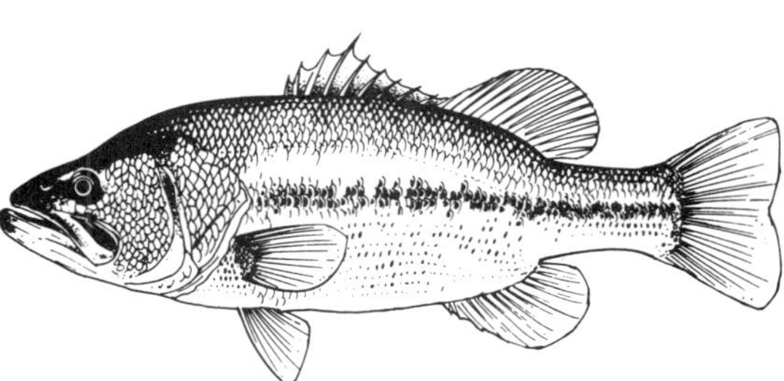

largemouth bass
114

Pacific ridley turtle
115

great frigate bird
116

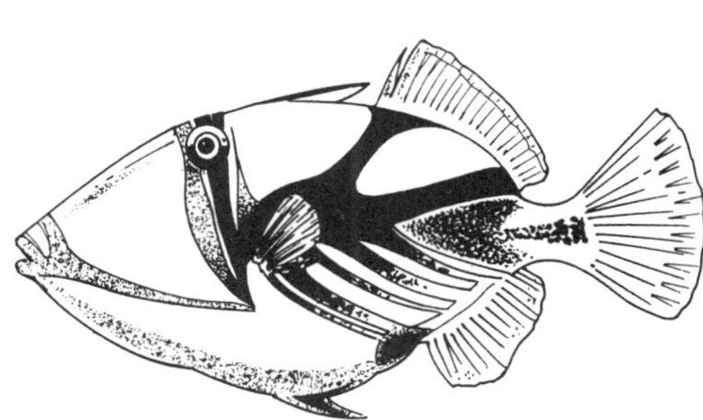

Picasso triggerfish
117

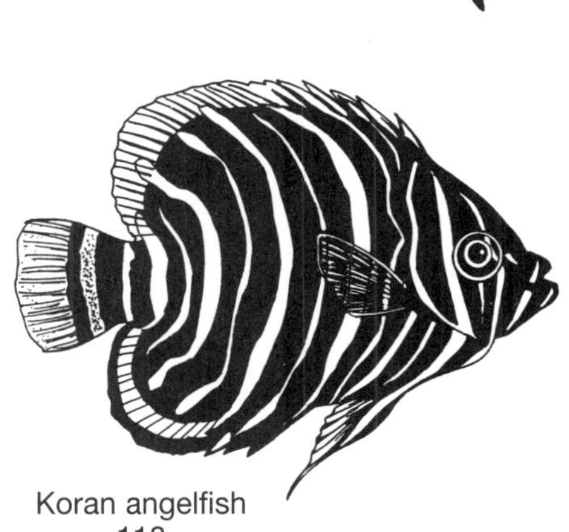

Koran angelfish
118

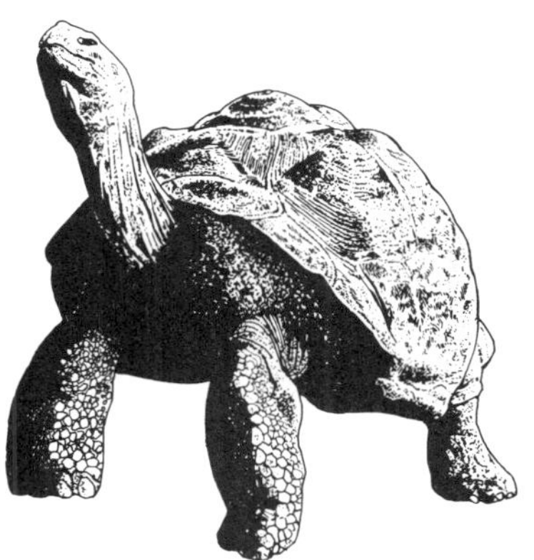

Galápagos tortoise
119

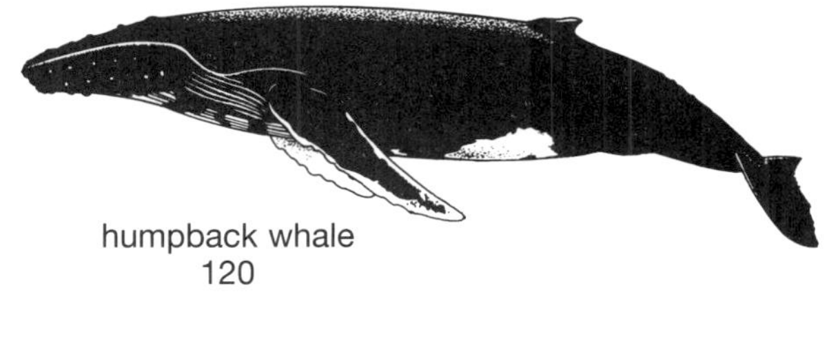

humpback whale
120

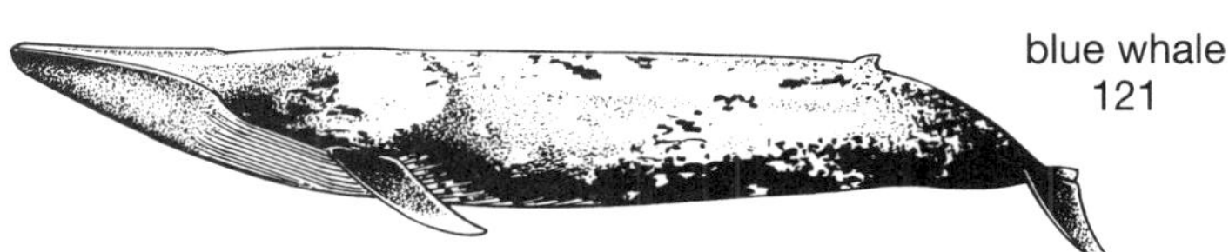

blue whale
121

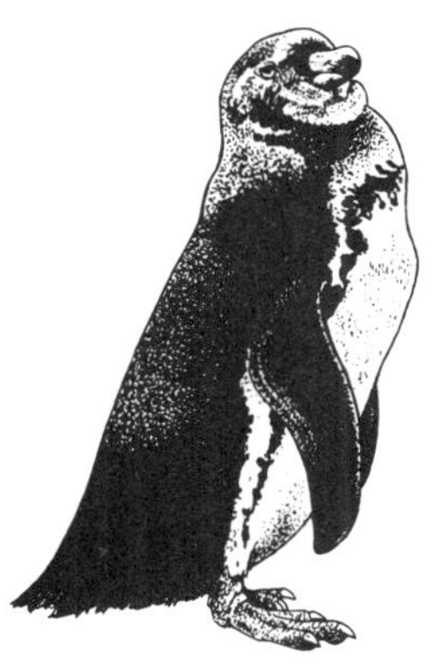

Galápagos penguin
122

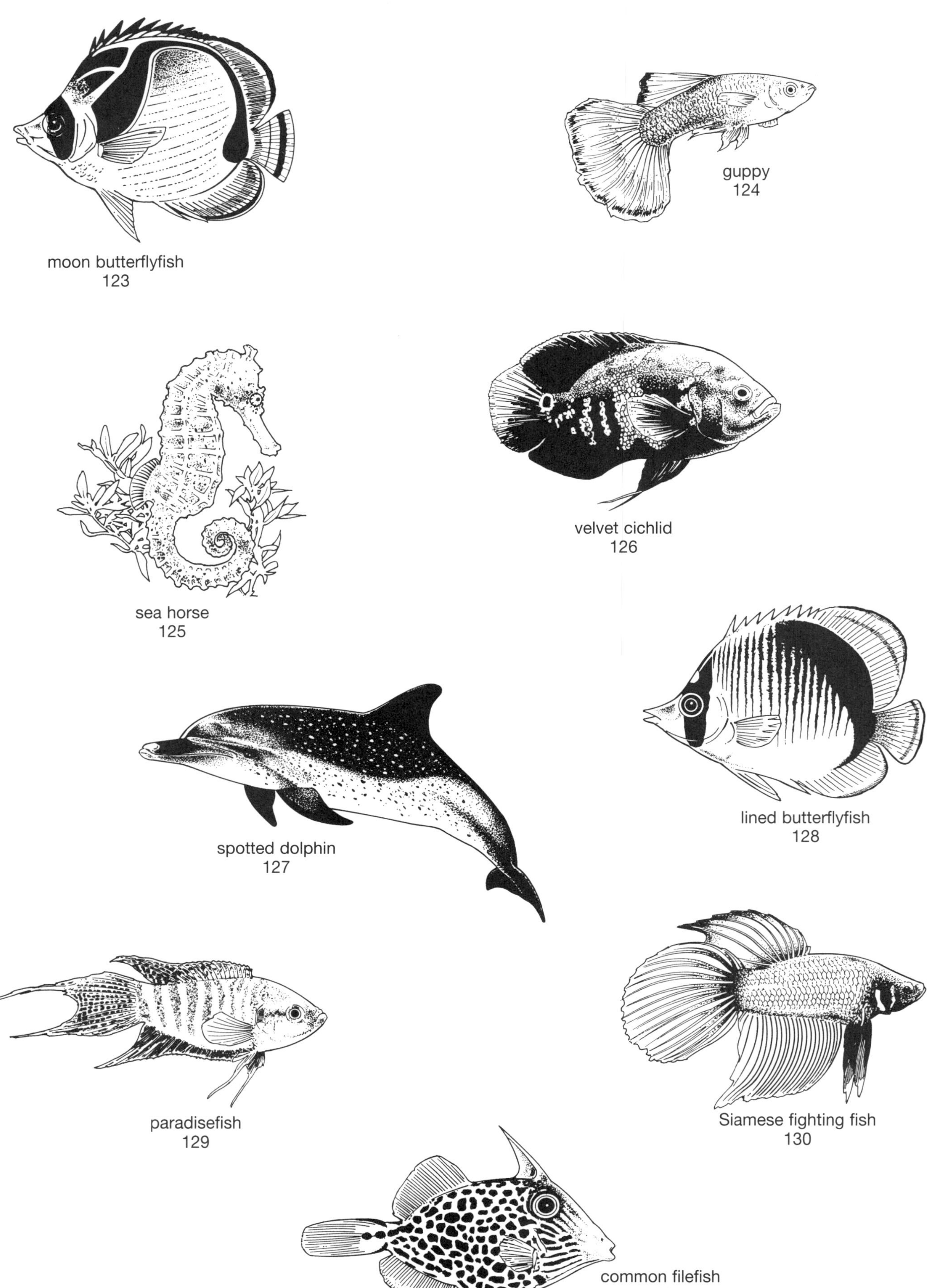

moon butterflyfish
123

guppy
124

sea horse
125

velvet cichlid
126

spotted dolphin
127

lined butterflyfish
128

paradisefish
129

Siamese fighting fish
130

common filefish
131

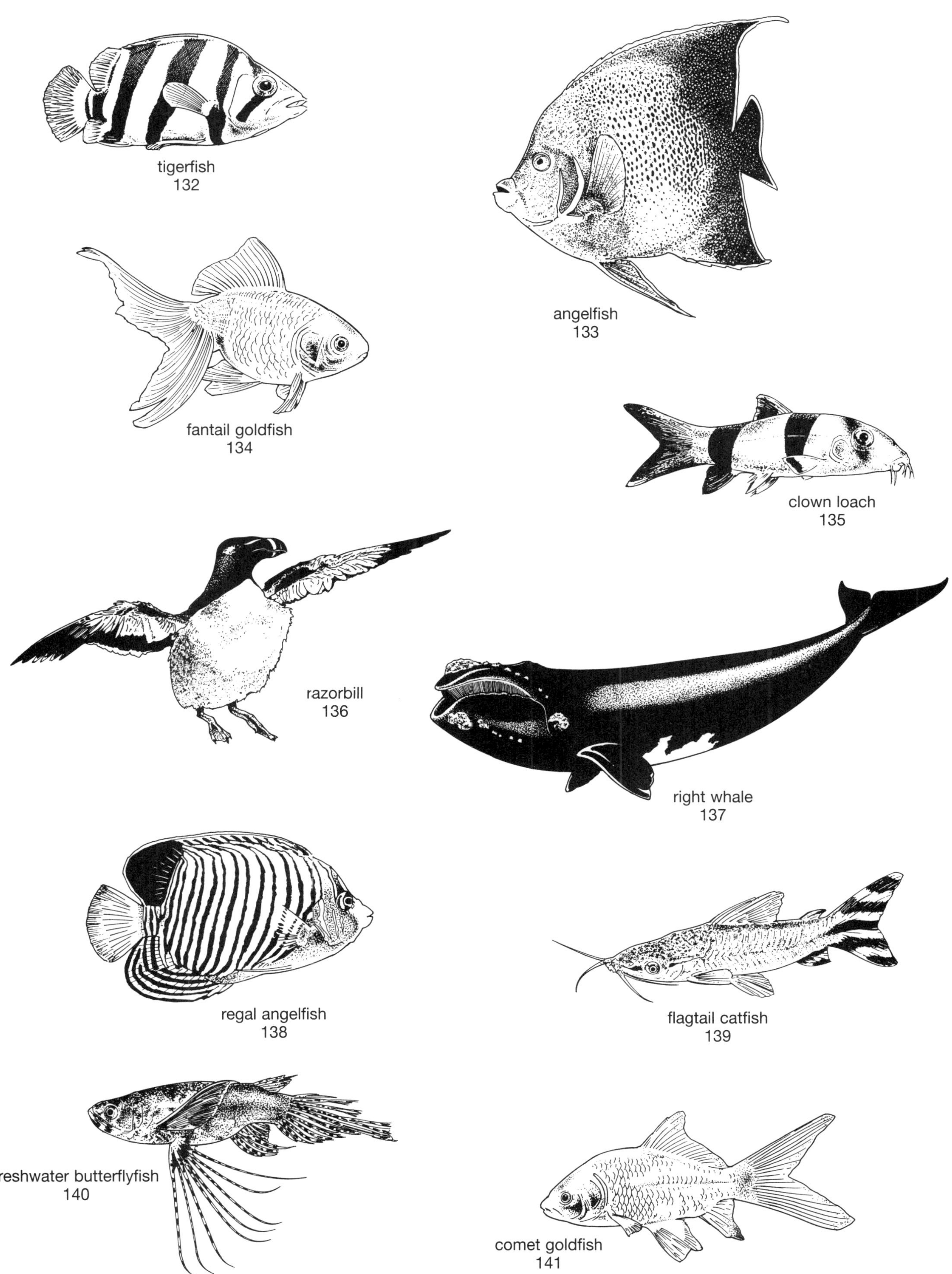
tigerfish
132
angelfish
133
fantail goldfish
134
clown loach
135
razorbill
136
right whale
137
regal angelfish
138
flagtail catfish
139
freshwater butterflyfish
140
comet goldfish
141

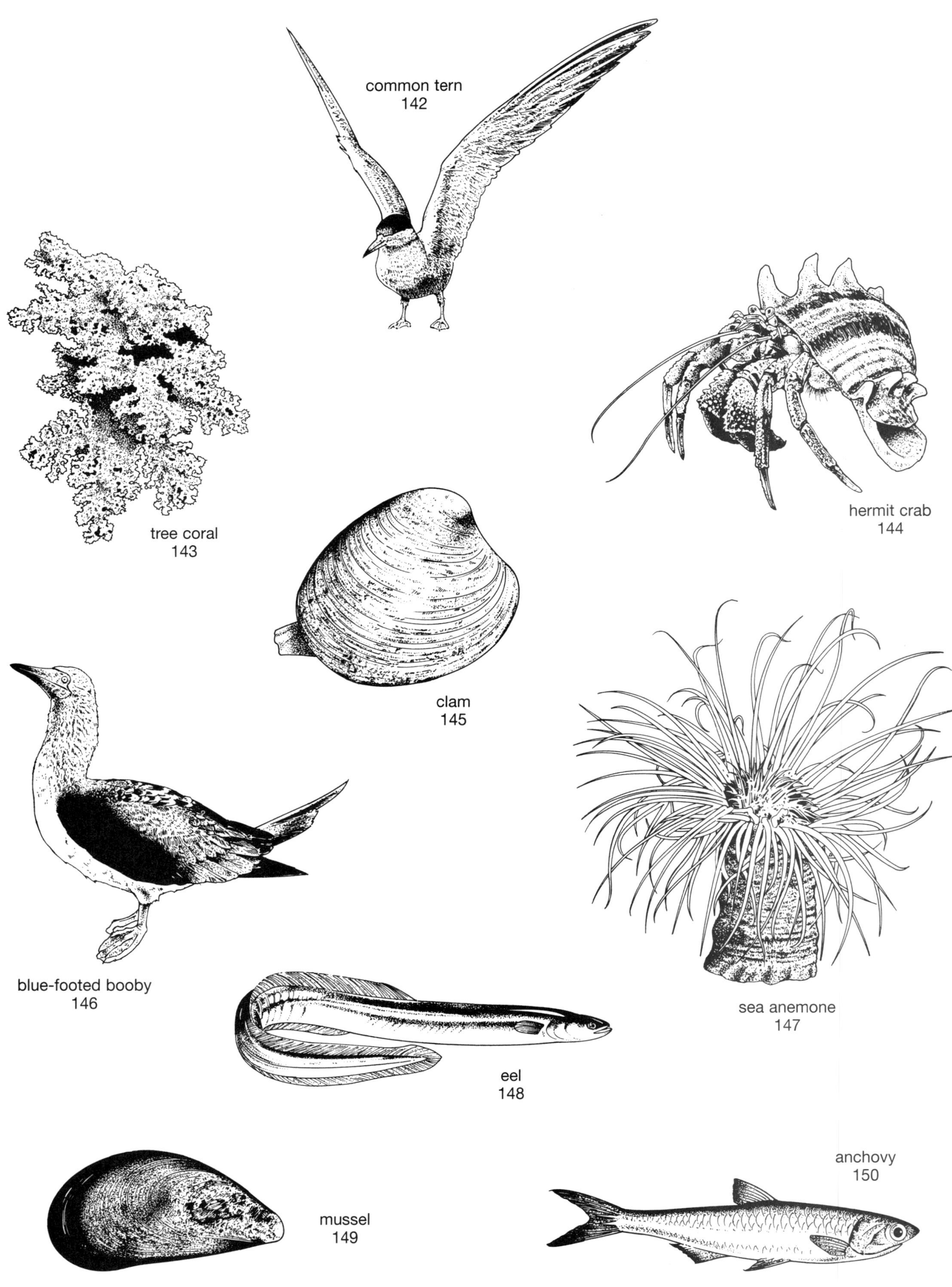
common tern
142
tree coral
143
hermit crab
144
clam
145
blue-footed booby
146
sea anemone
147
eel
148
mussel
149
anchovy
150

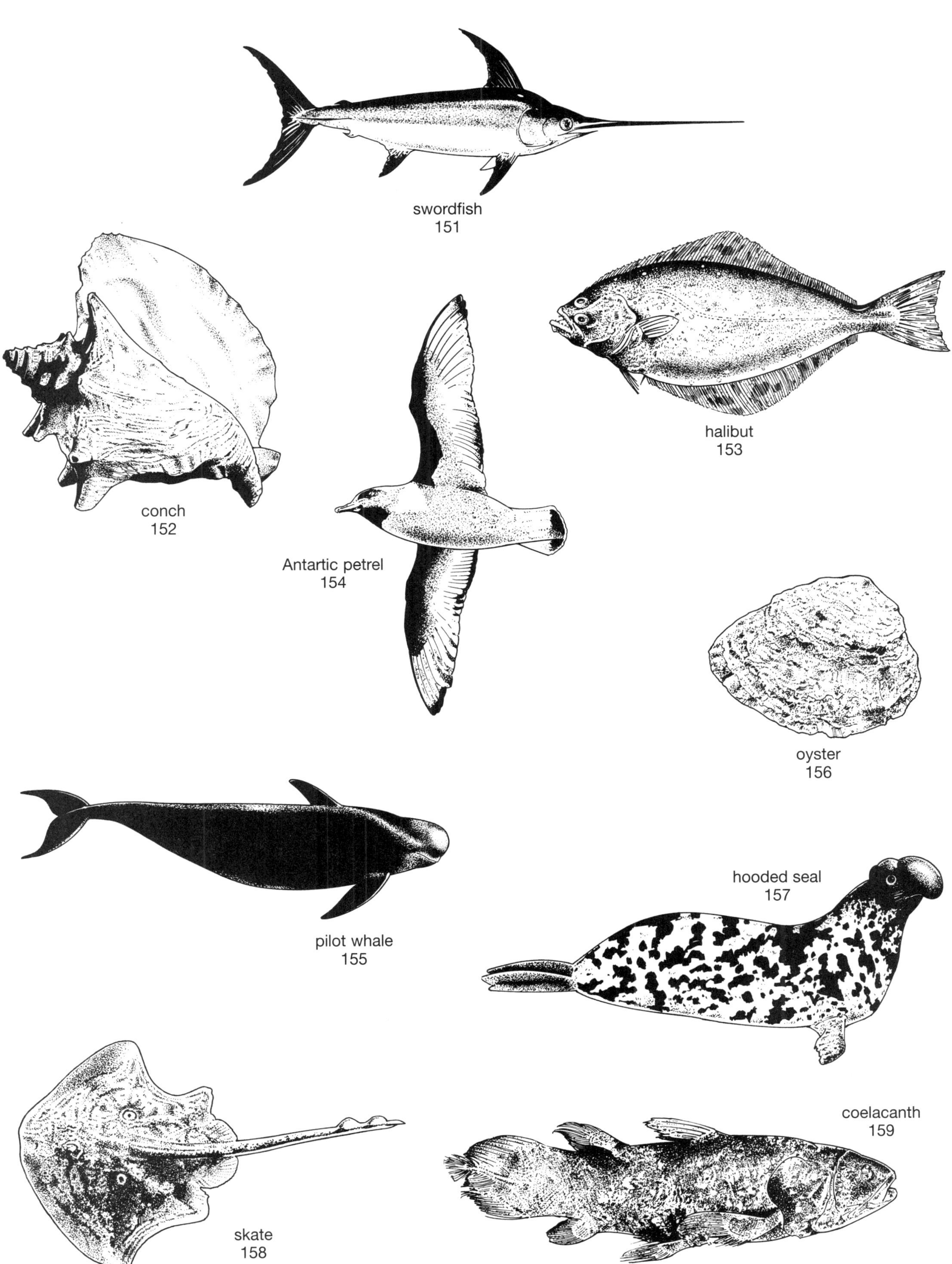
swordfish
151
conch
152
halibut
153
Antartic petrel
154
oyster
156
pilot whale
155
hooded seal
157
coelacanth
159
skate
158

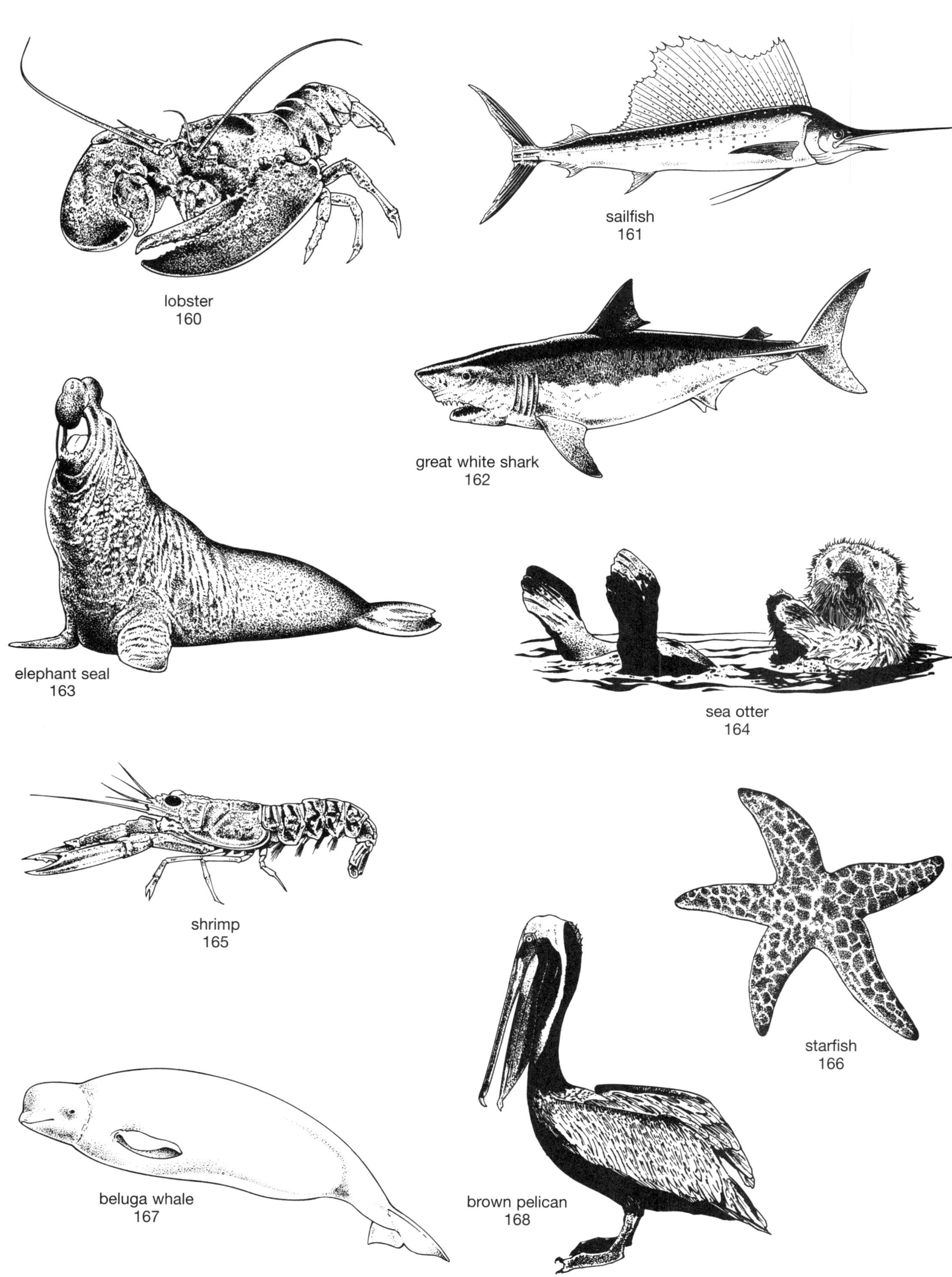

lobster
160

sailfish
161

great white shark
162

elephant seal
163

sea otter
164

shrimp
165

starfish
166

beluga whale
167

brown pelican
168

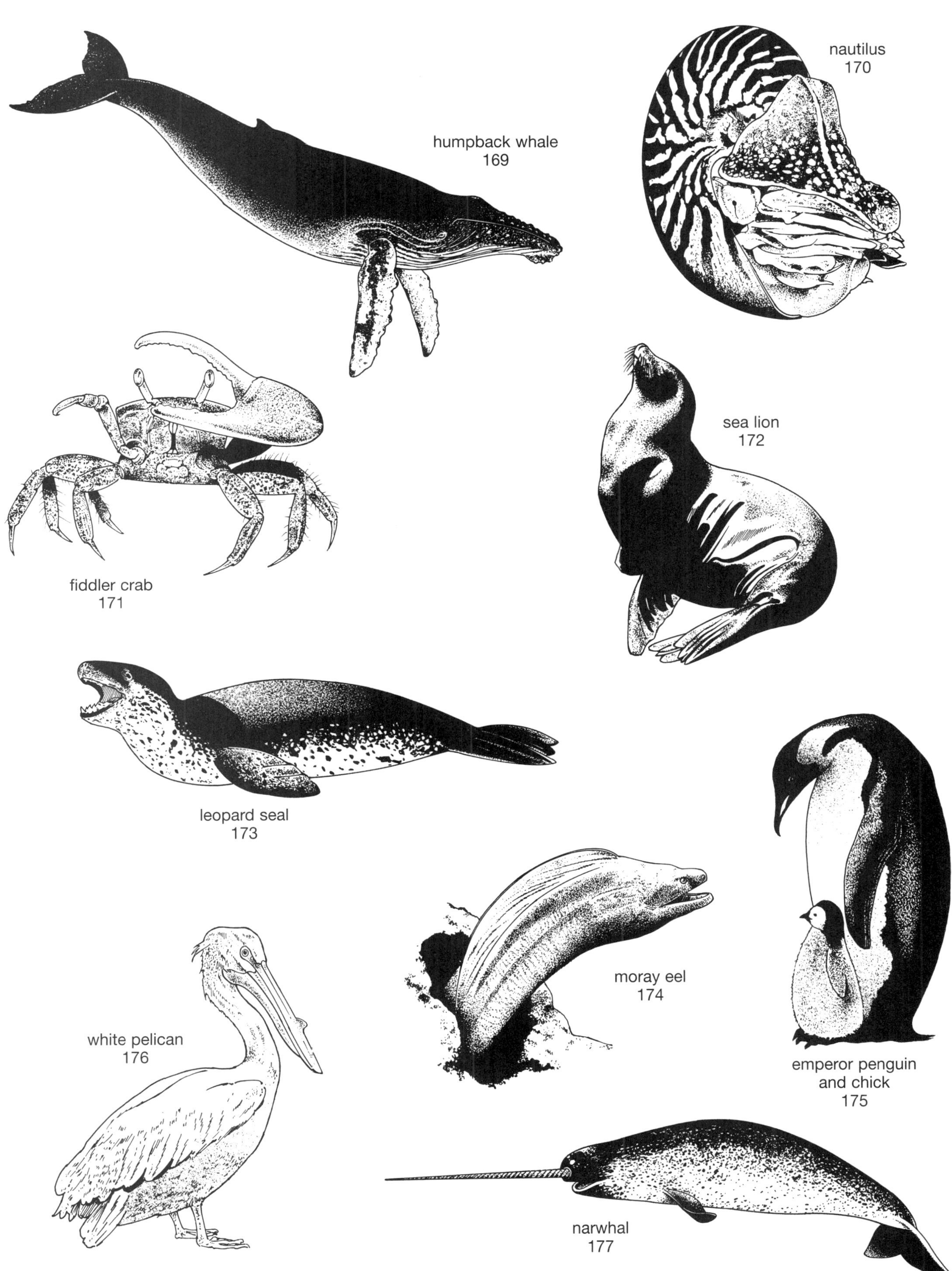
humpback whale
169
nautilus
170
fiddler crab
171
sea lion
172
leopard seal
173
moray eel
174
emperor penguin
and chick
175
white pelican
176
narwhal
177

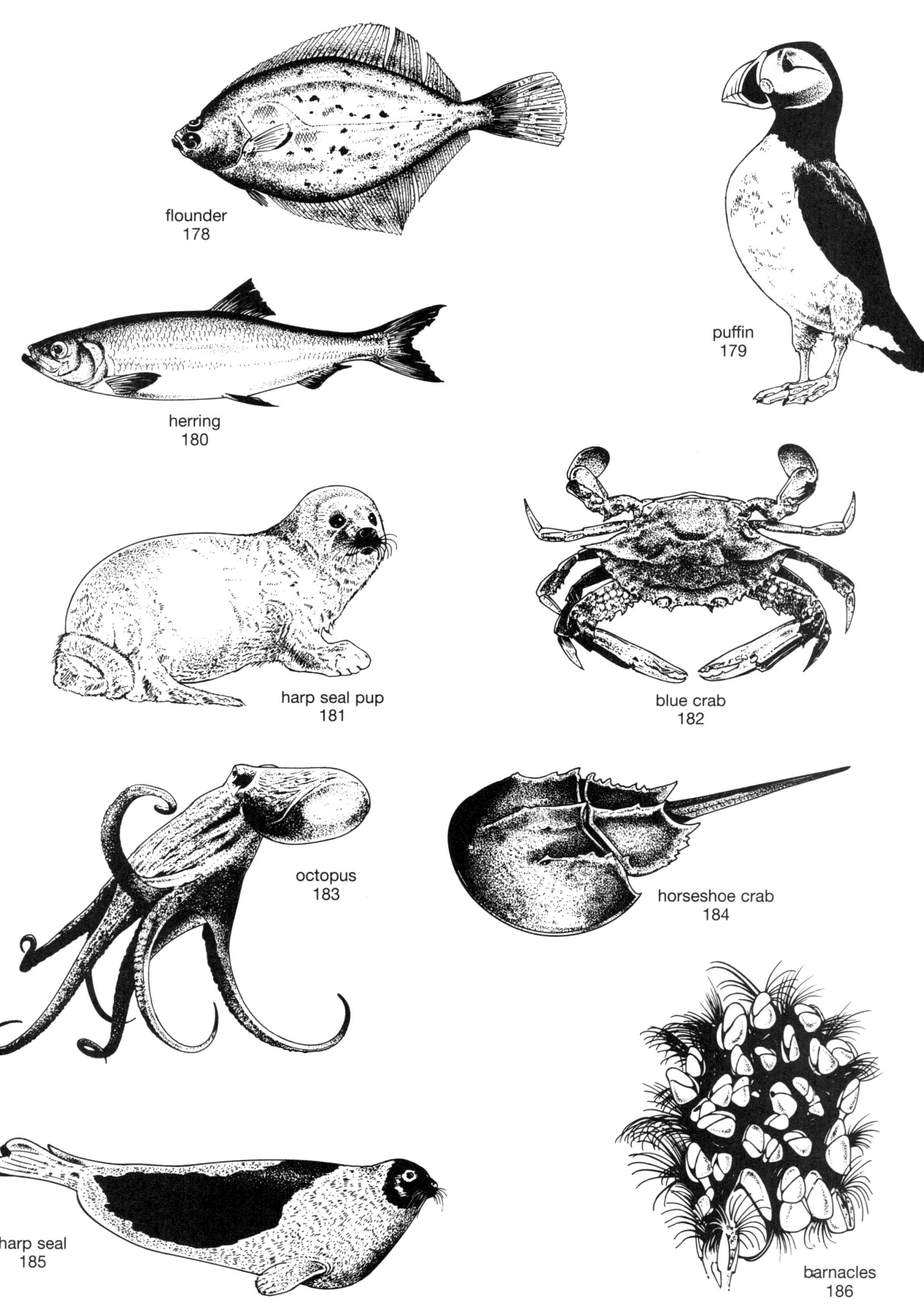
flounder
178
puffin
179
herring
180
harp seal pup
181
blue crab
182
octopus
183
horseshoe crab
184
harp seal
185
barnacles
186

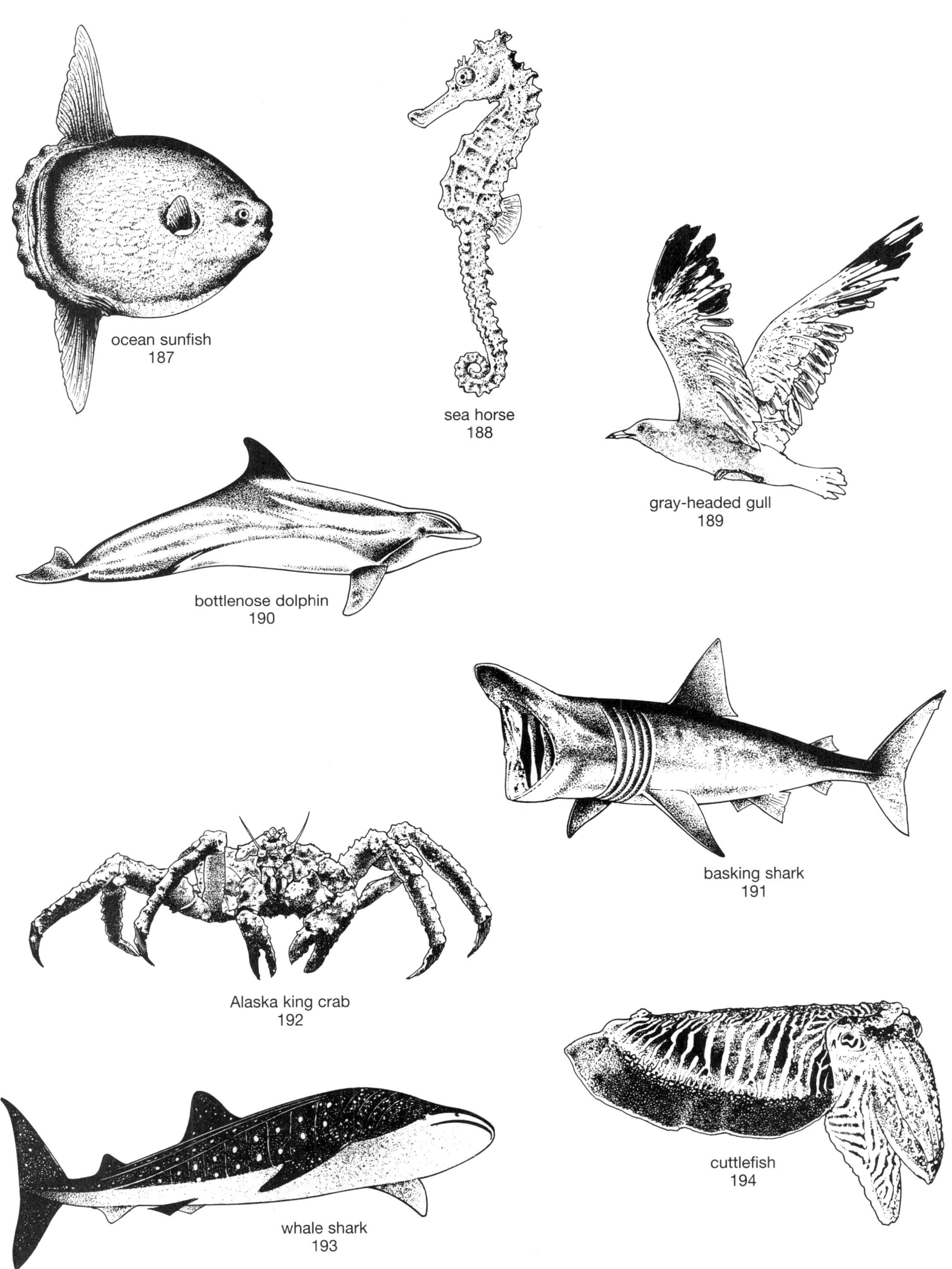
ocean sunfish
187

sea horse
188

gray-headed gull
189

bottlenose dolphin
190

basking shark
191

Alaska king crab
192

whale shark
193

cuttlefish
194

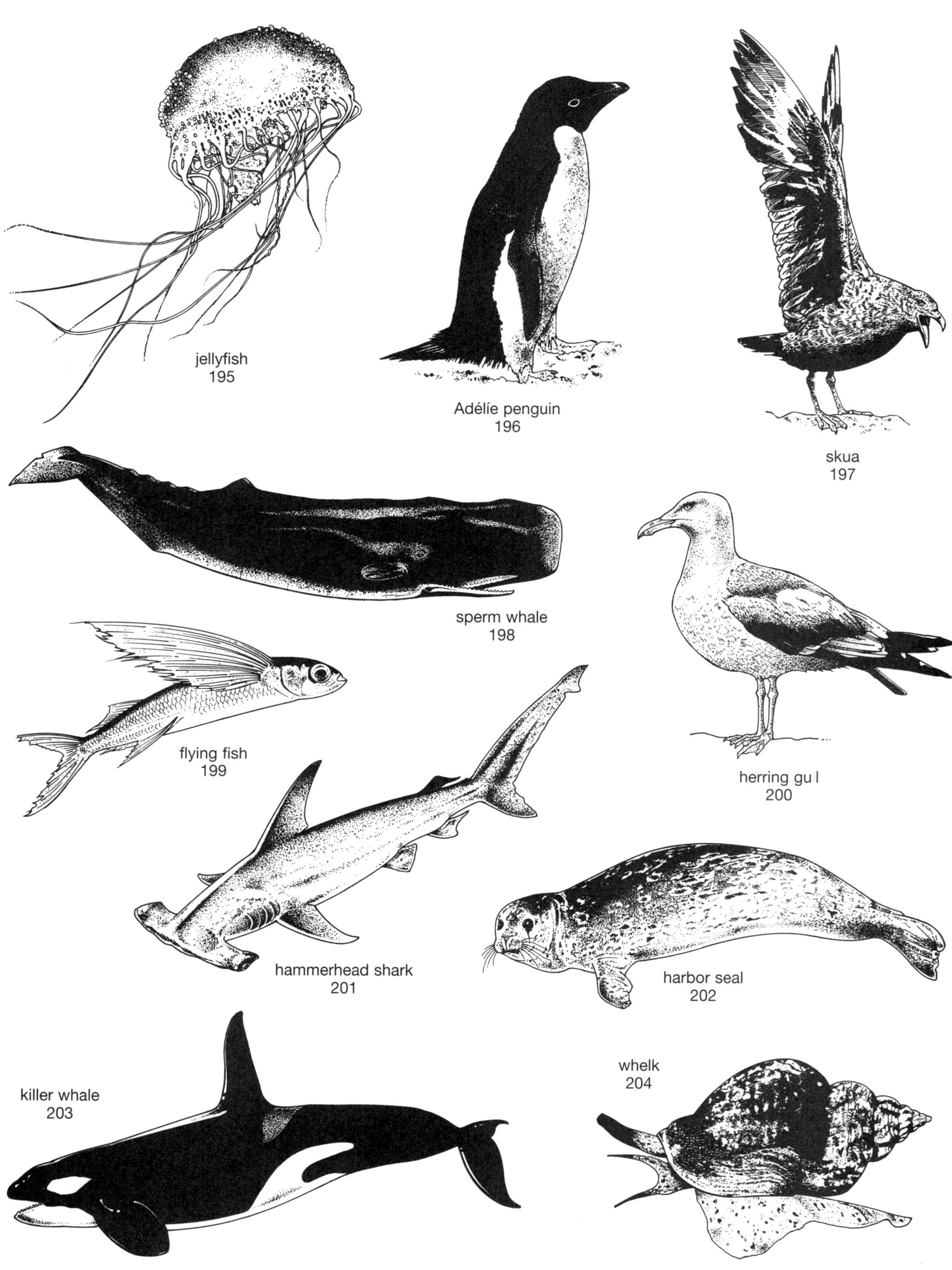
jellyfish
195
Adélie penguin
196
skua
197
sperm whale
198
flying fish
199
herring gull
200
hammerhead shark
201
harbor seal
202
killer whale
203
whelk
204

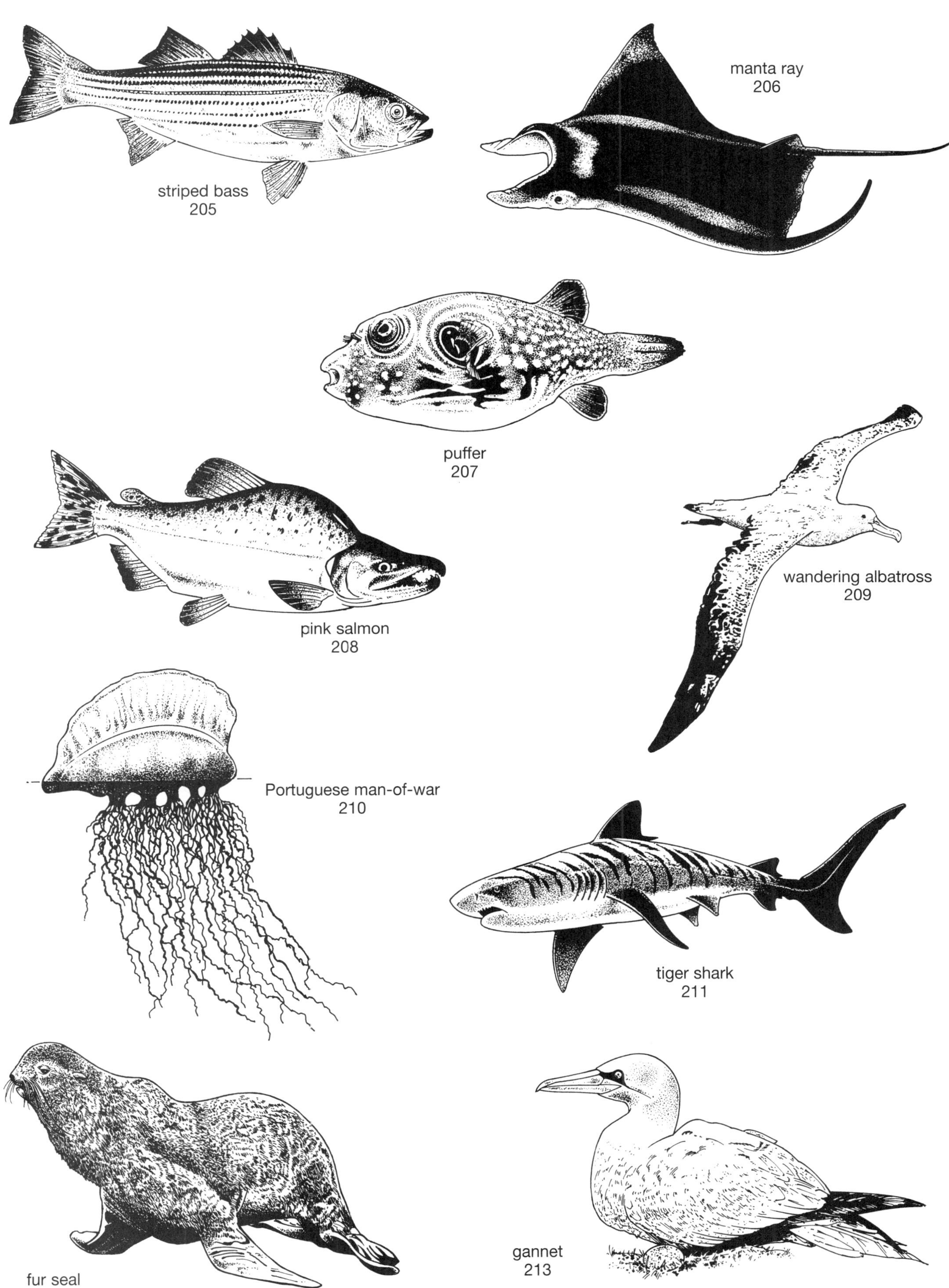
striped bass
205
manta ray
206
puffer
207
pink salmon
208
wandering albatross
209
Portuguese man-of-war
210
tiger shark
211
fur seal
212
gannet
213

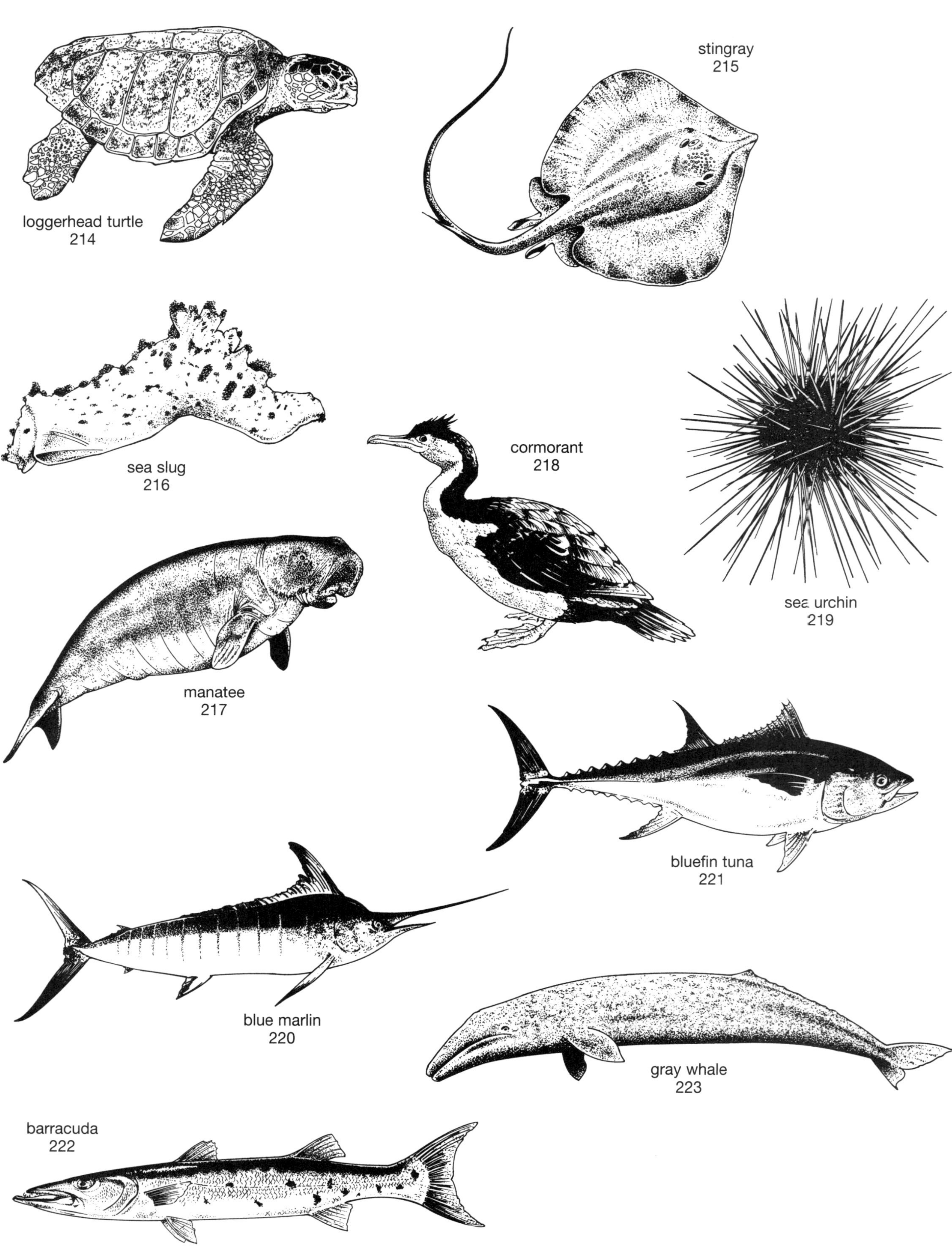
loggerhead turtle
214
stingray
215
sea slug
216
cormorant
218
sea urchin
219
manatee
217
bluefin tuna
221
blue marlin
220
gray whale
223
barracuda
222

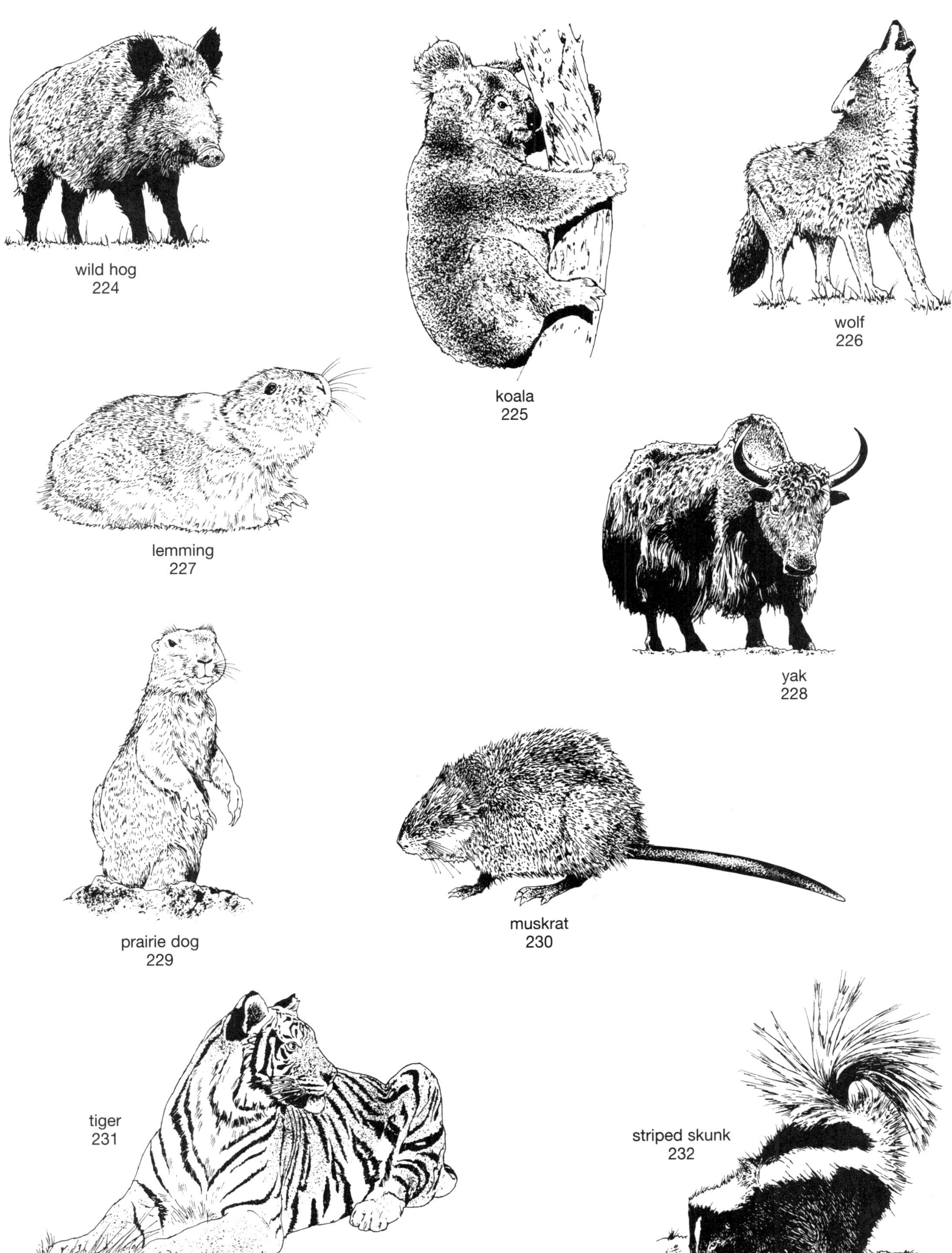
wild hog
224
koala
225
wolf
226
lemming
227
yak
228
prairie dog
229
muskrat
230
tiger
231
striped skunk
232

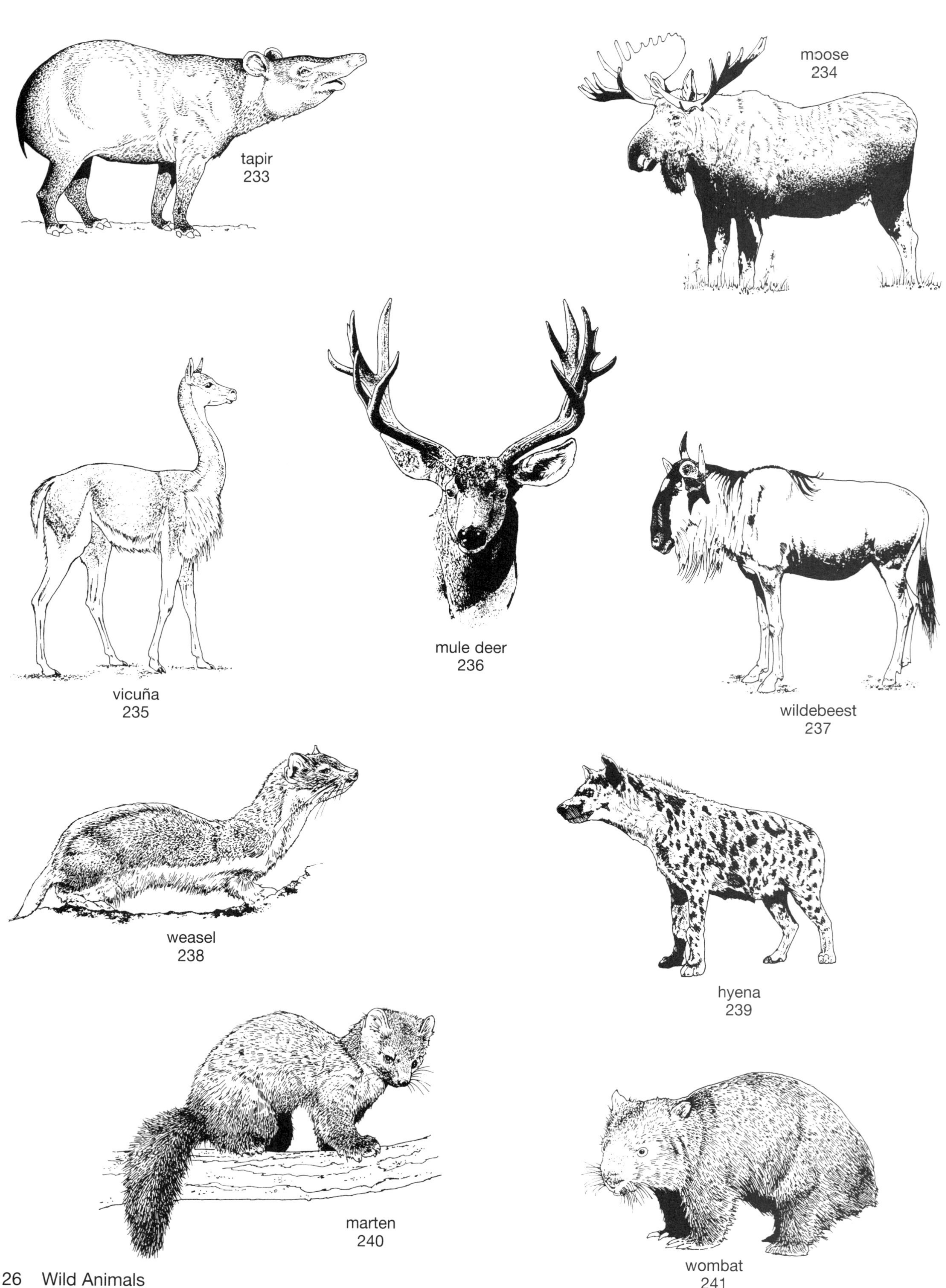
tapir
233
moose
234
vicuña
235
mule deer
236
wildebeest
237
weasel
238
hyena
239
marten
240
wombat
241

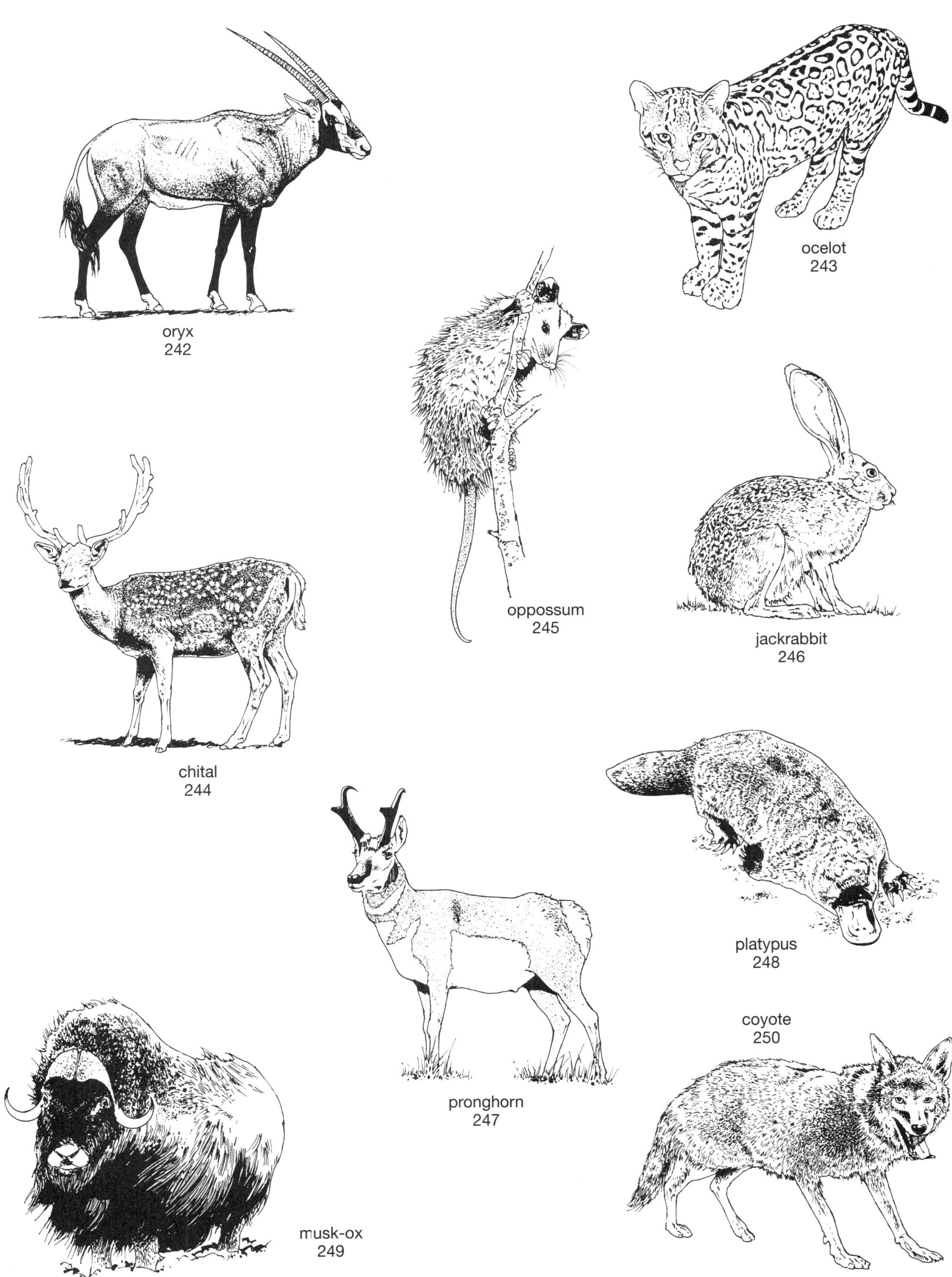
oryx
242
ocelot
243
chital
244
oppossum
245
jackrabbit
246
pronghorn
247
platypus
248
musk-ox
249
coyote
250

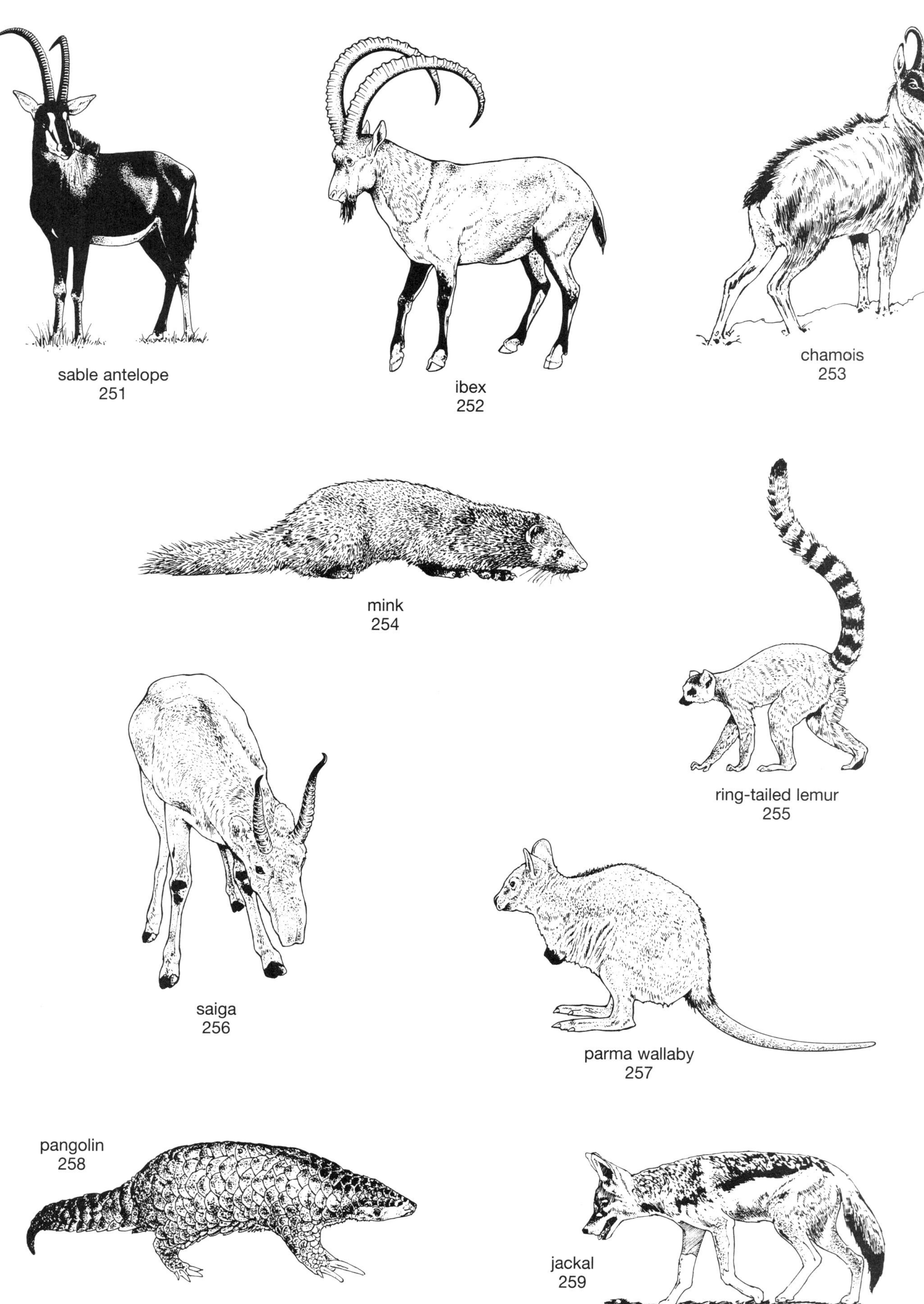
sable antelope
251
ibex
252
chamois
253
mink
254
ring-tailed lemur
255
saiga
256
parma wallaby
257
pangolin
258
jackal
259

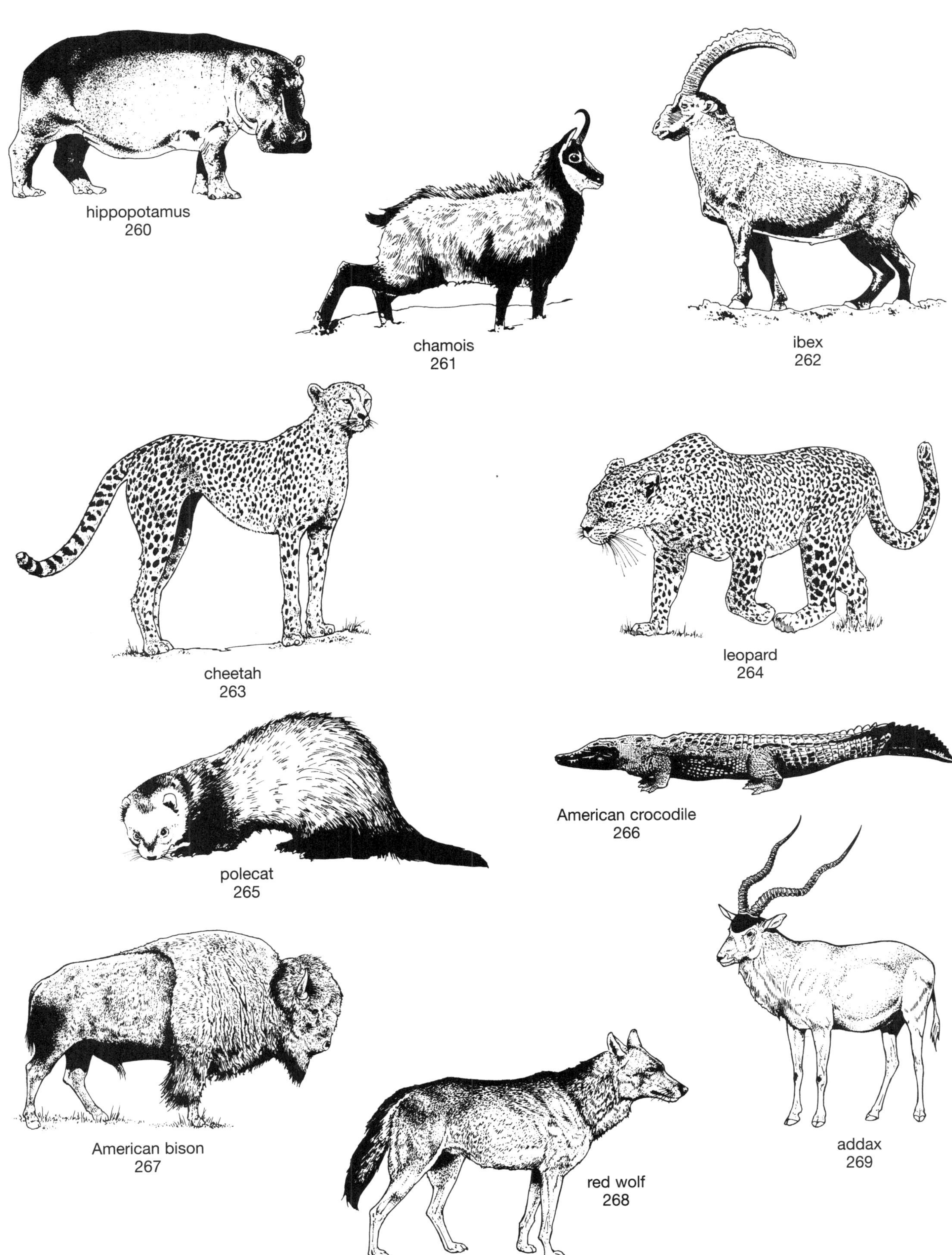
hippopotamus
260
chamois
261
ibex
262
cheetah
263
leopard
264
polecat
265
American crocodile
266
American bison
267
red wolf
268
addax
269

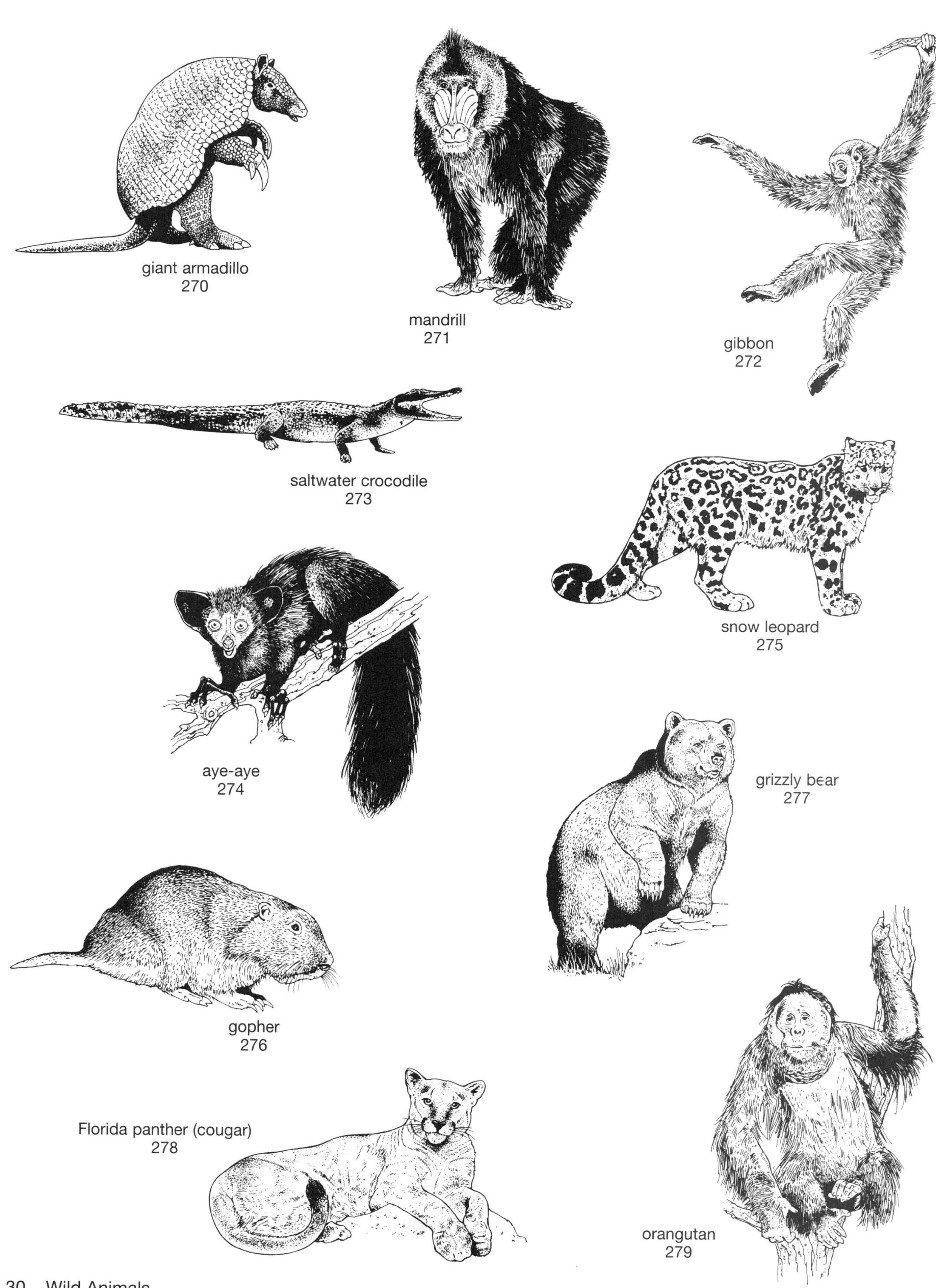
giant armadillo
270
mandrill
271
gibbon
272
saltwater crocodile
273
snow leopard
275
aye-aye
274
grizzly bear
277
gopher
276
Florida panther (cougar)
278
orangutan
279

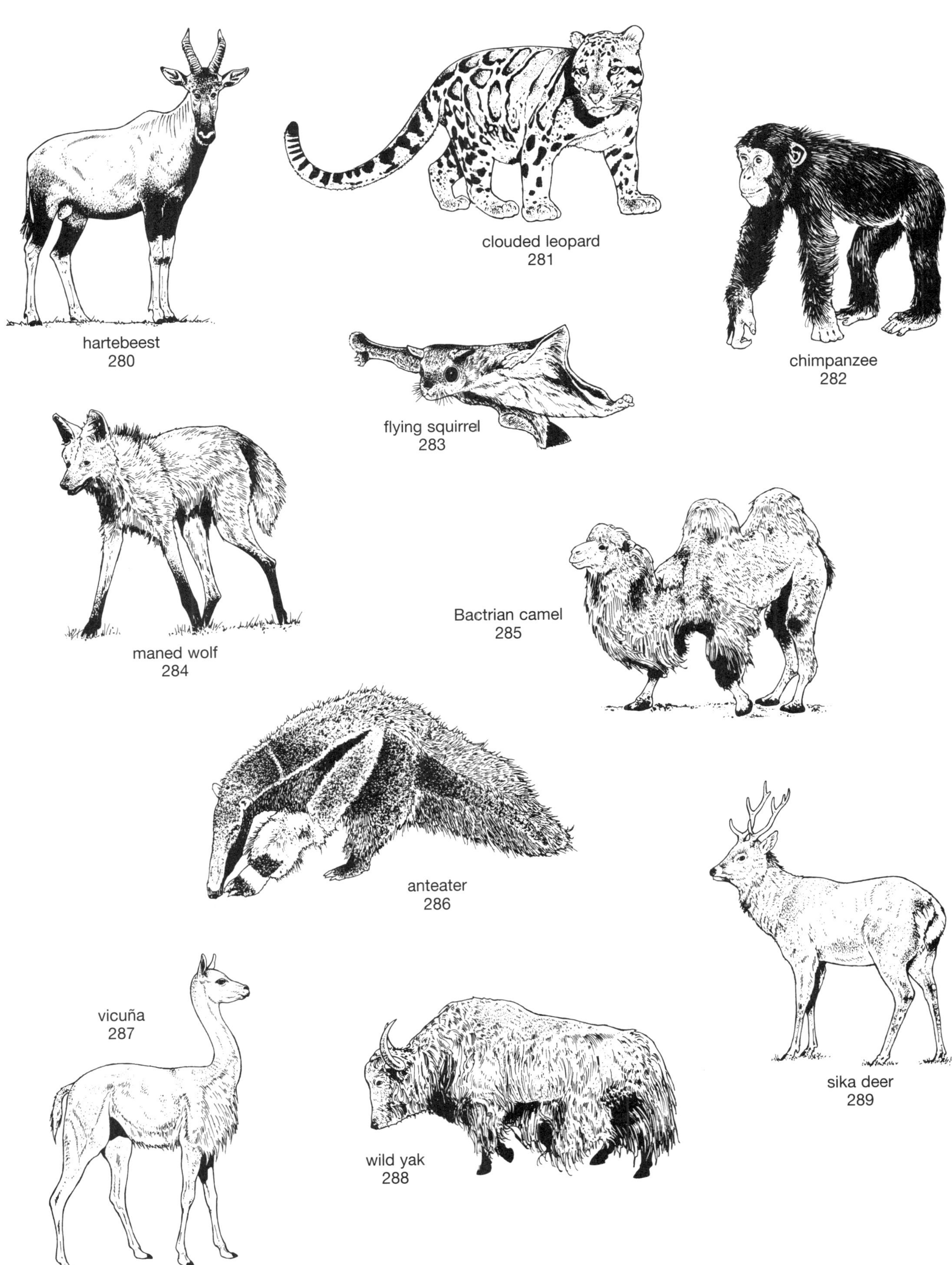
hartebeest
280
clouded leopard
281
chimpanzee
282
flying squirrel
283
maned wolf
284
Bactrian camel
285
anteater
286
vicuña
287
wild yak
288
sika deer
289

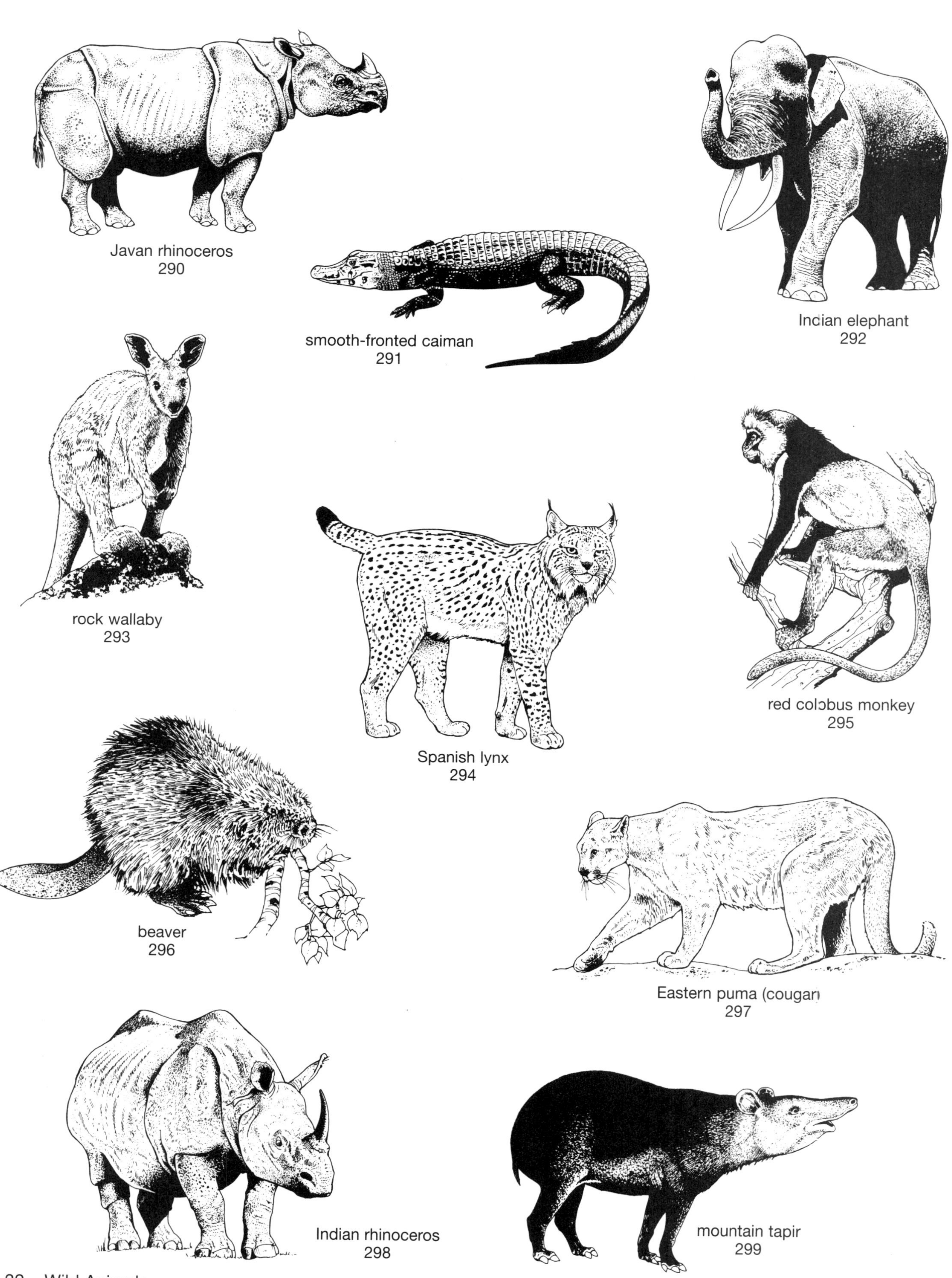

Javan rhinoceros
290

smooth-fronted caiman
291

Indian elephant
292

rock wallaby
293

Spanish lynx
294

red colobus monkey
295

beaver
296

Eastern puma (cougar)
297

Indian rhinoceros
298

mountain tapir
299

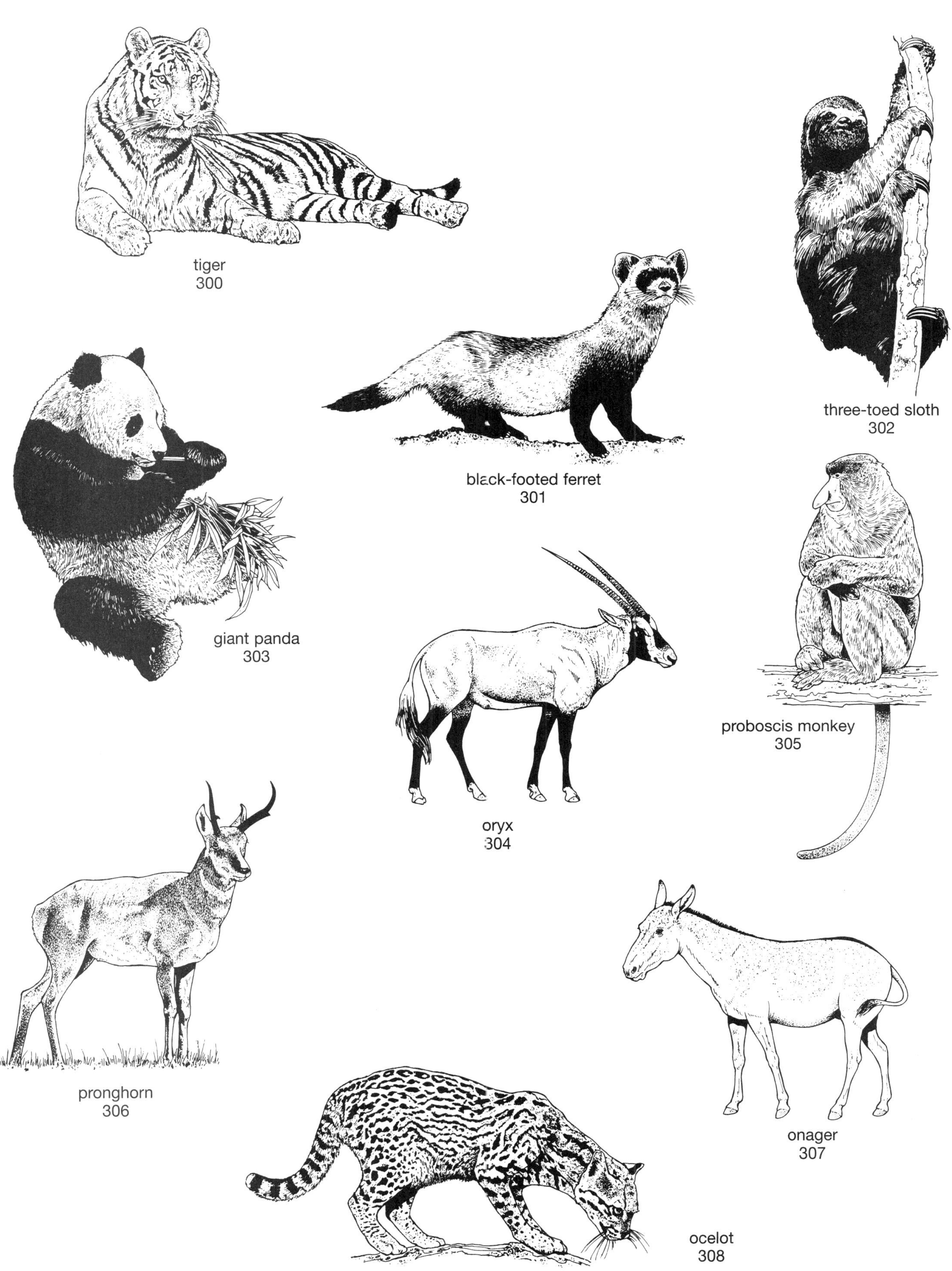
tiger
300
black-footed ferret
301
three-toed sloth
302
giant panda
303
oryx
304
proboscis monkey
305
pronghorn
306
onager
307
ocelot
308

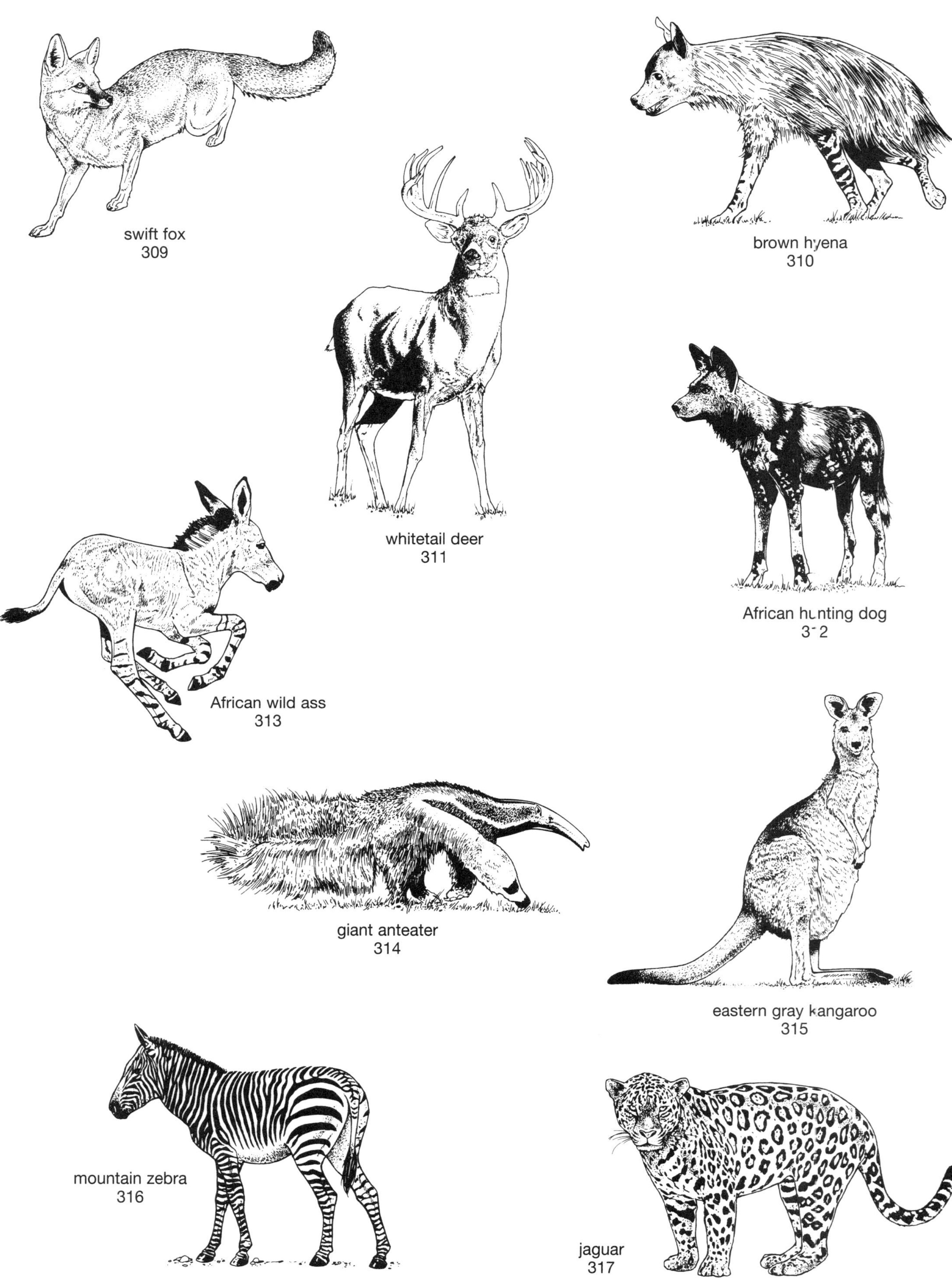

swift fox
309

brown hyena
310

whitetail deer
311

African hunting dog
312

African wild ass
313

giant anteater
314

eastern gray kangaroo
315

mountain zebra
316

jaguar
317

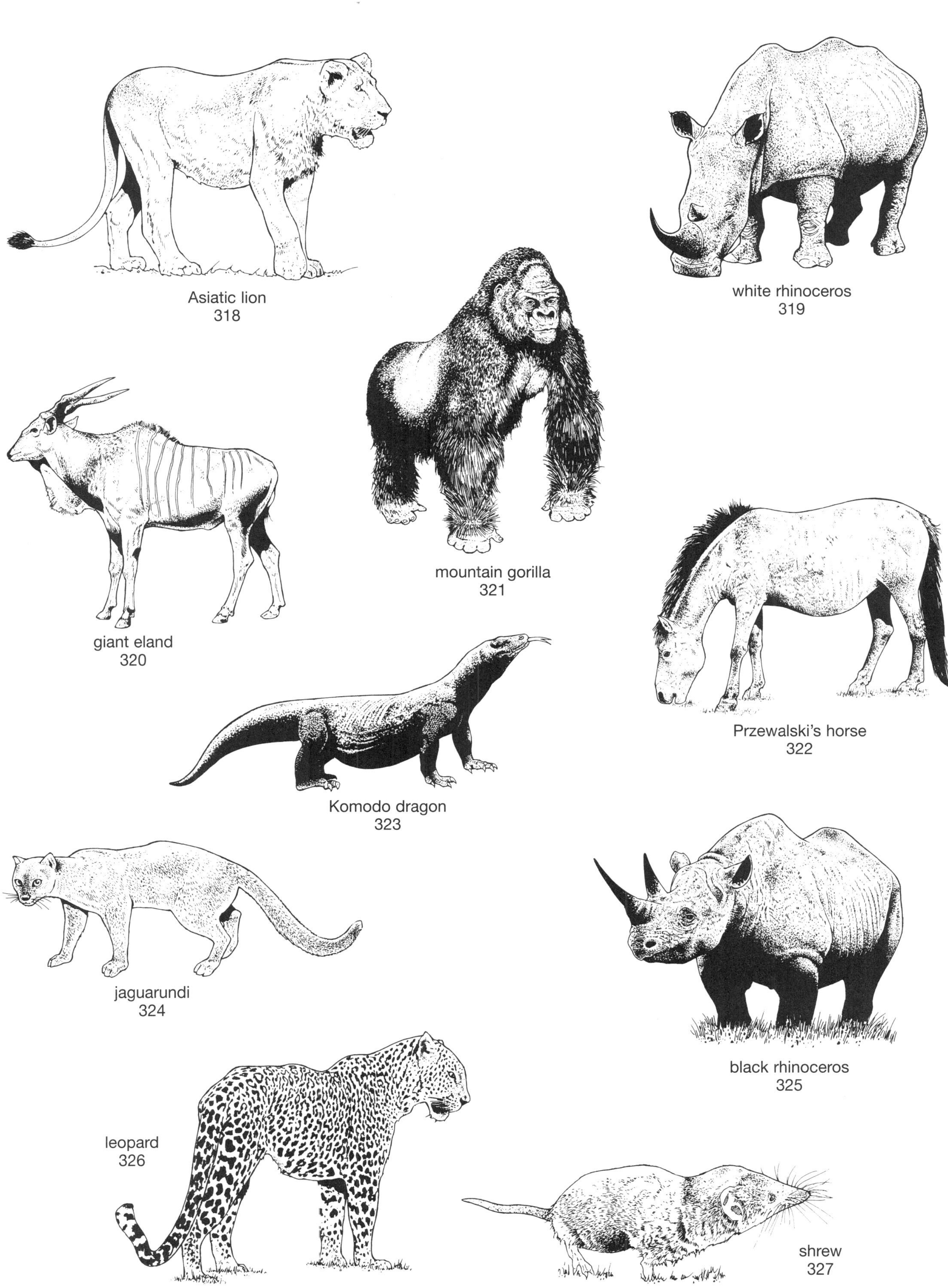
Asiatic lion
318
white rhinoceros
319
mountain gorilla
321
giant eland
320
Przewalski's horse
322
Komodo dragon
323
jaguarundi
324
black rhinoceros
325
leopard
326
shrew
327

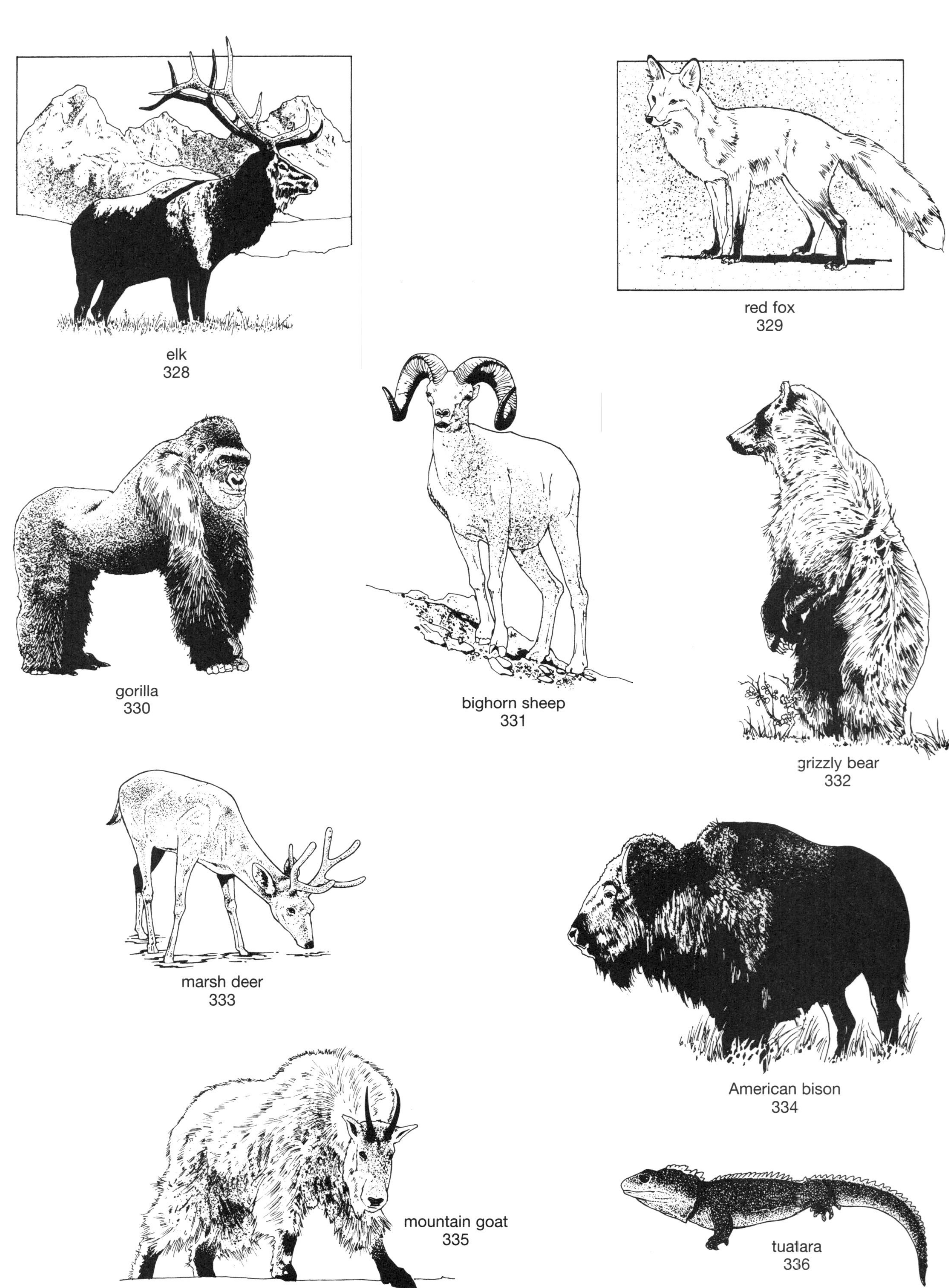
elk
328
red fox
329
gorilla
330
bighorn sheep
331
grizzly bear
332
marsh deer
333
American bison
334
mountain goat
335
tuatara
336

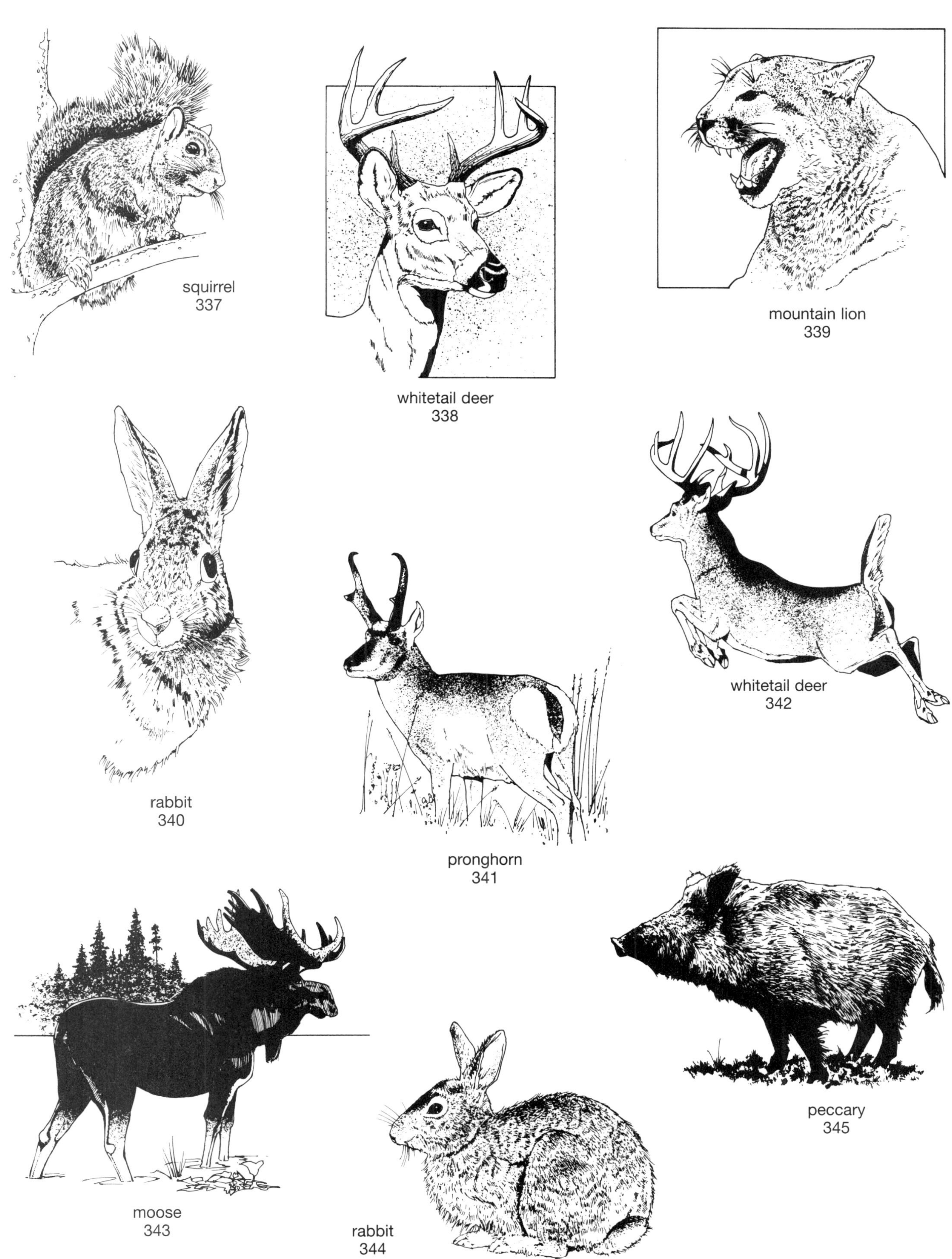

squirrel
337

whitetail deer
338

mountain lion
339

rabbit
340

pronghorn
341

whitetail deer
342

moose
343

rabbit
344

peccary
345

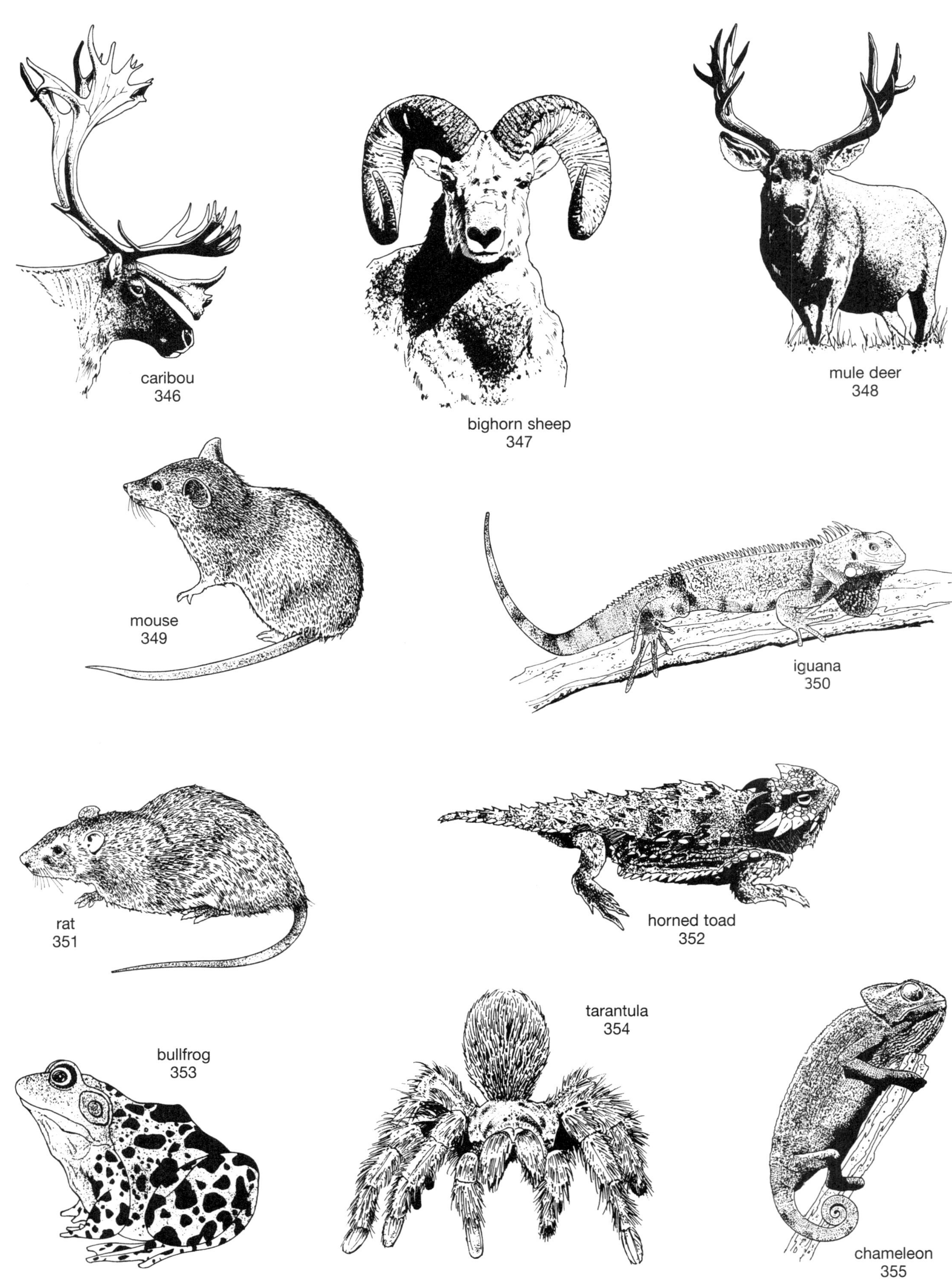
caribou
346
bighorn sheep
347
mule deer
348
mouse
349
iguana
350
rat
351
horned toad
352
bullfrog
353
tarantula
354
chameleon
355

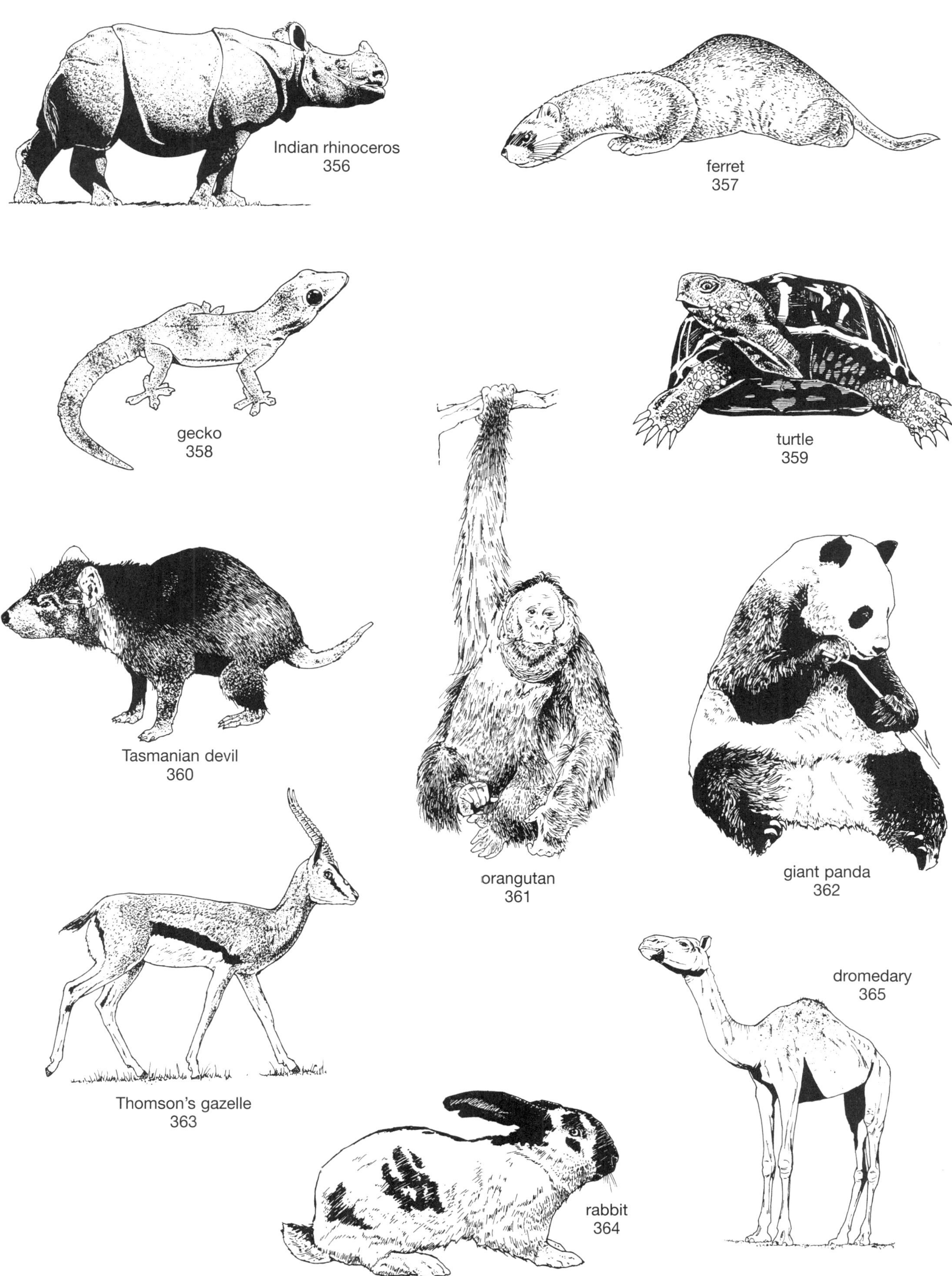
Indian rhinoceros
356
ferret
357
gecko
358
turtle
359
Tasmanian devil
360
orangutan
361
giant panda
362
Thomson's gazelle
363
rabbit
364
dromedary
365

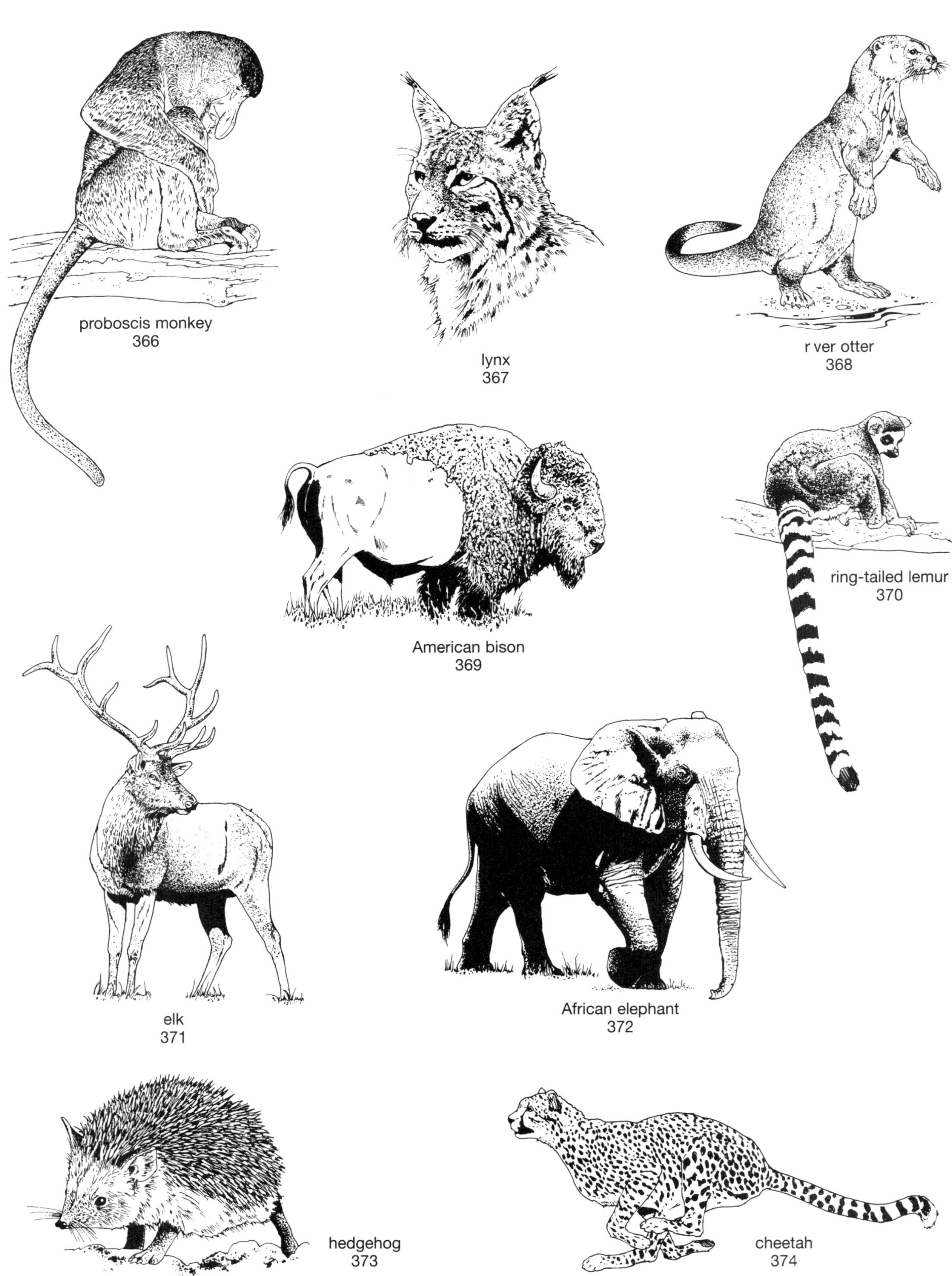
proboscis monkey
366
lynx
367
r ver otter
368
American bison
369
ring-tailed lemur
370
elk
371
African elephant
372
hedgehog
373
cheetah
374

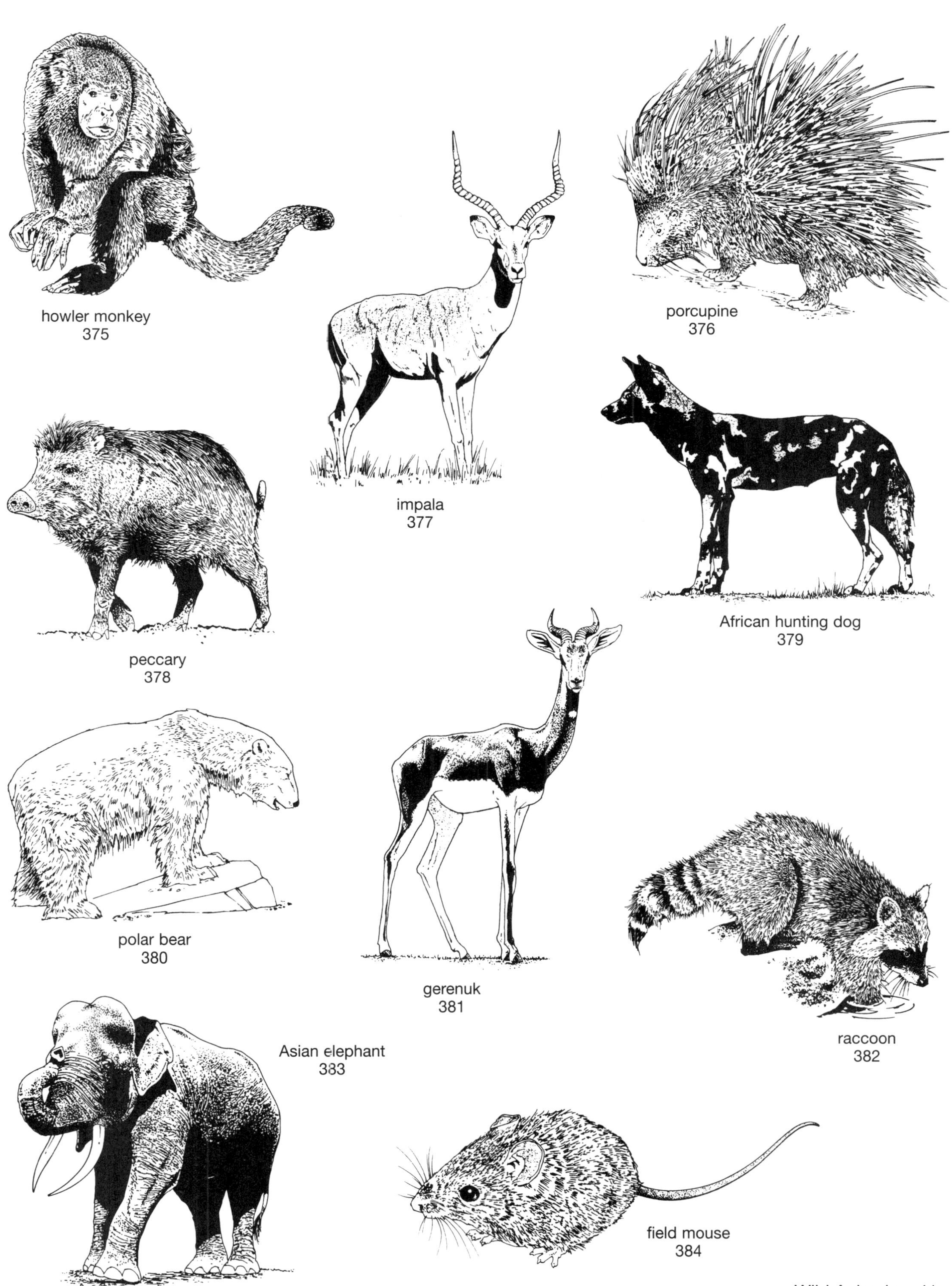

howler monkey
375
porcupine
376
impala
377
peccary
378
African hunting dog
379
polar bear
380
gerenuk
381
raccoon
382
Asian elephant
383
field mouse
384

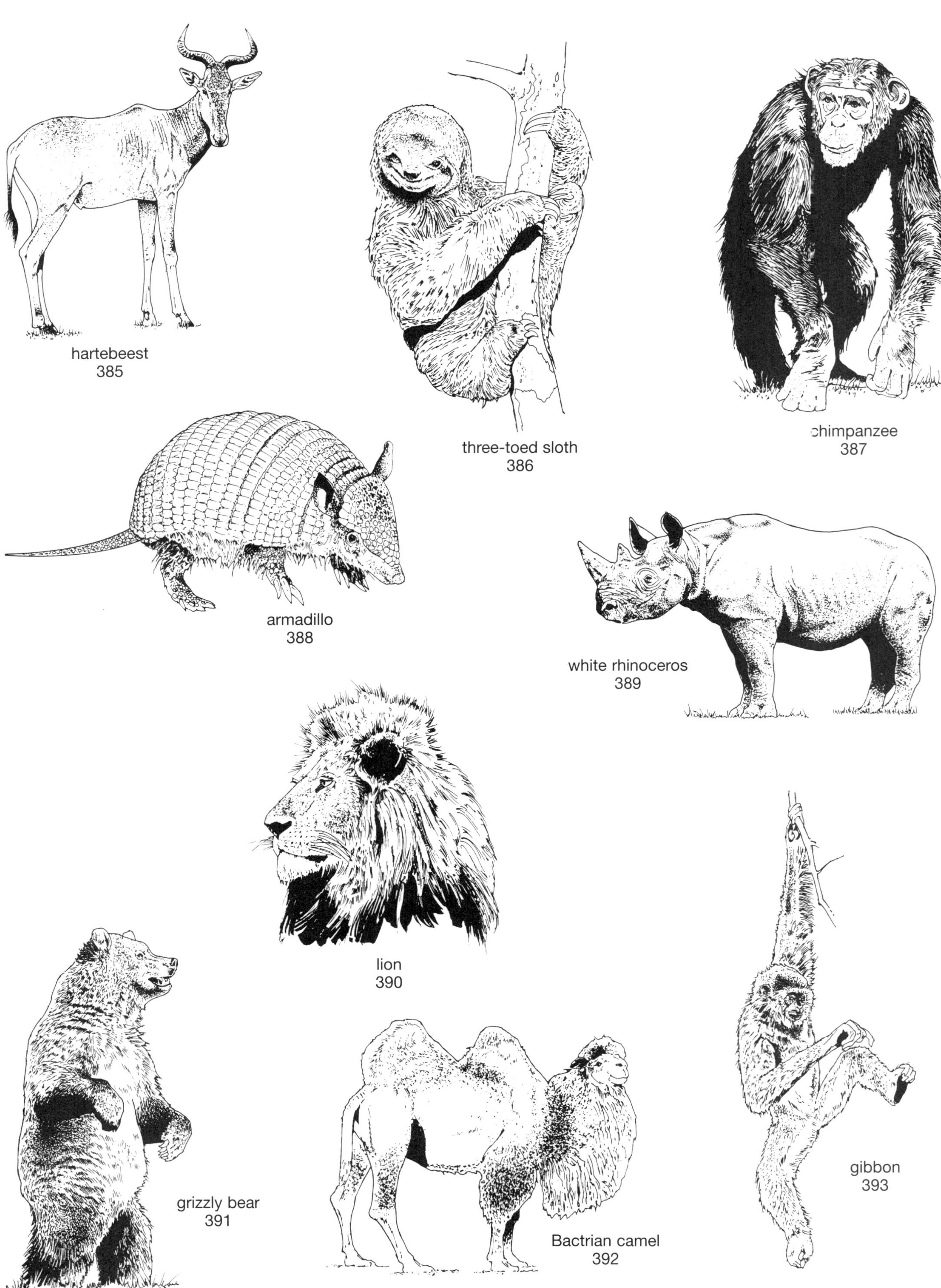
hartebeest
385
three-toed sloth
386
chimpanzee
387
armadillo
388
white rhinoceros
389
lion
390
grizzly bear
391
Bactrian camel
392
gibbon
393

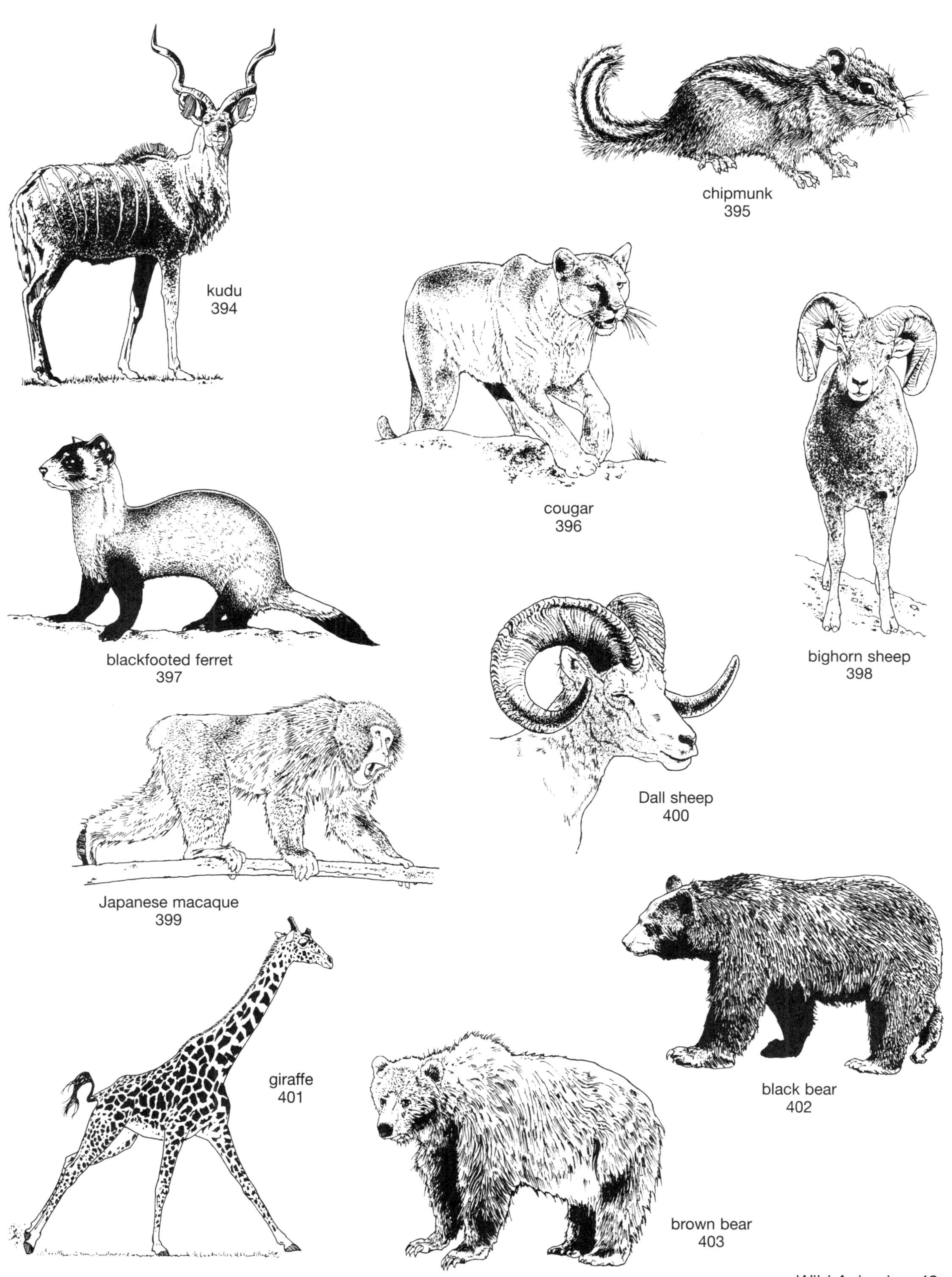
kudu
394
chipmunk
395
cougar
396
blackfooted ferret
397
bighorn sheep
398
Japanese macaque
399
Dall sheep
400
giraffe
401
black bear
402
brown bear
403

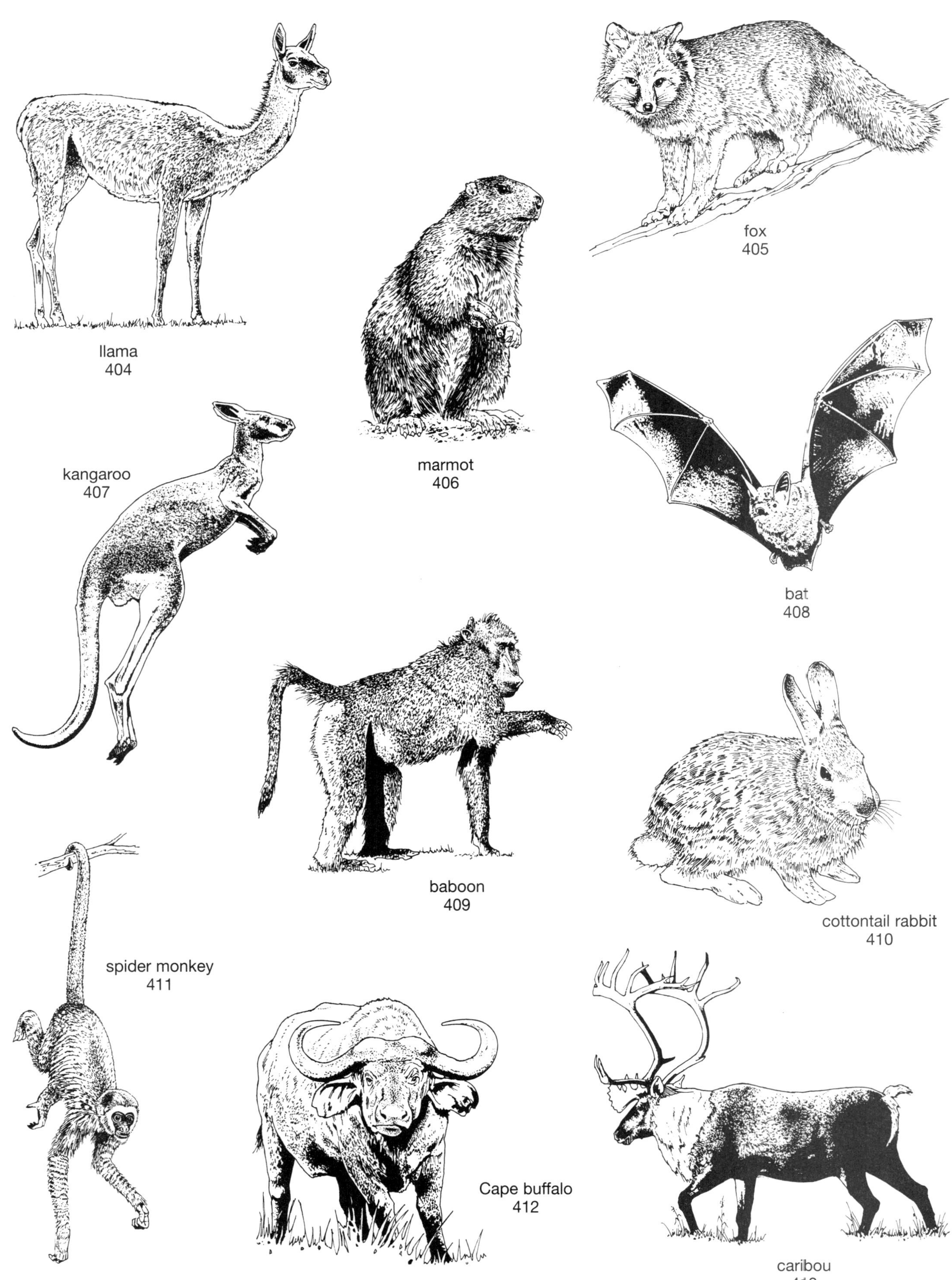
llama
404
fox
405
marmot
406
kangaroo
407
bat
408
baboon
409
cottontail rabbit
410
spider monkey
411
Cape buffalo
412
caribou
413

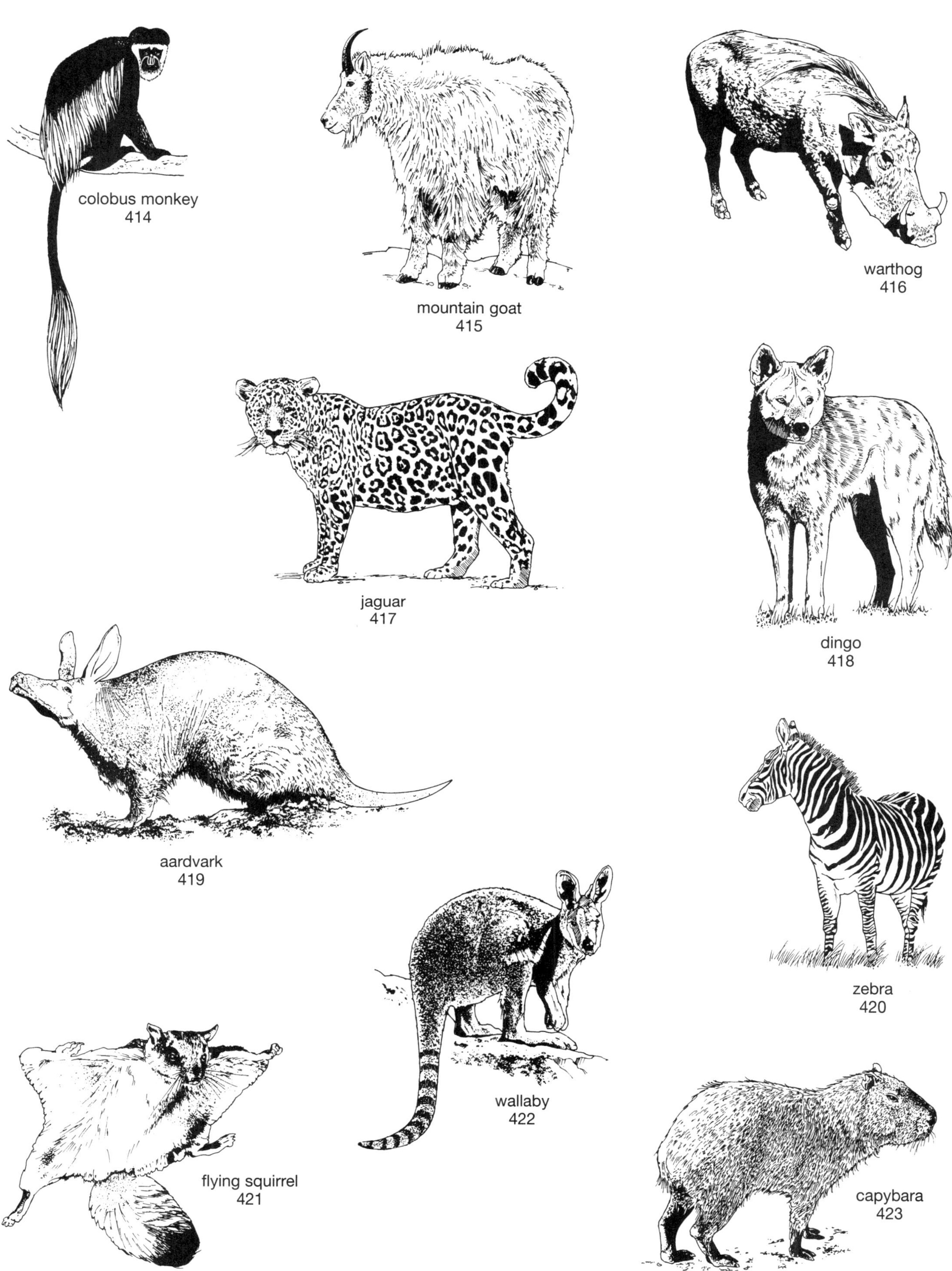
colobus monkey
414
mountain goat
415
warthog
416
jaguar
417
dingo
418
aardvark
419
zebra
420
flying squirrel
421
wallaby
422
capybara
423

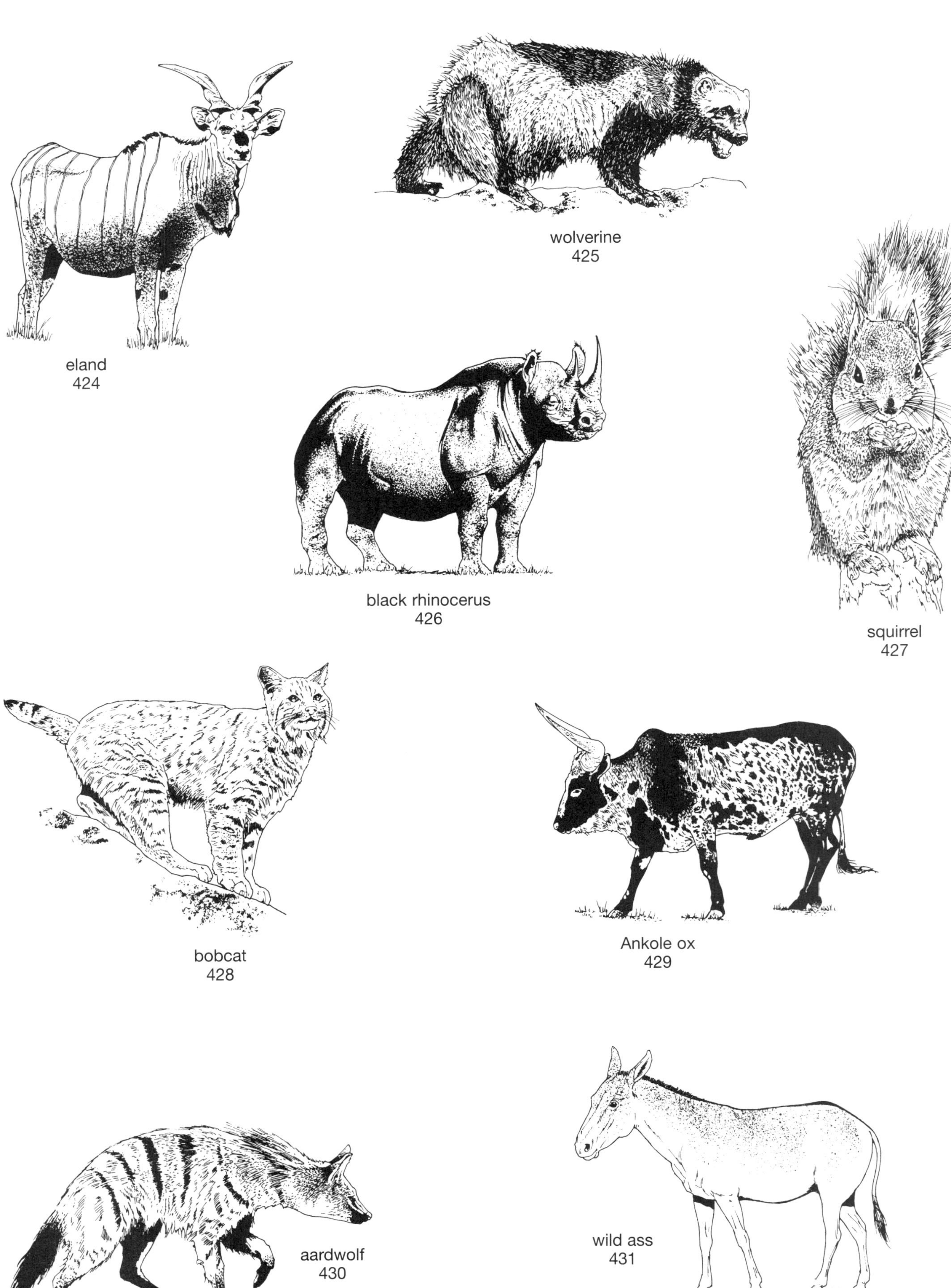
eland
424

wolverine
425

black rhinocerus
426

squirrel
427

bobcat
428

Ankole ox
429

aardwolf
430

wild ass
431

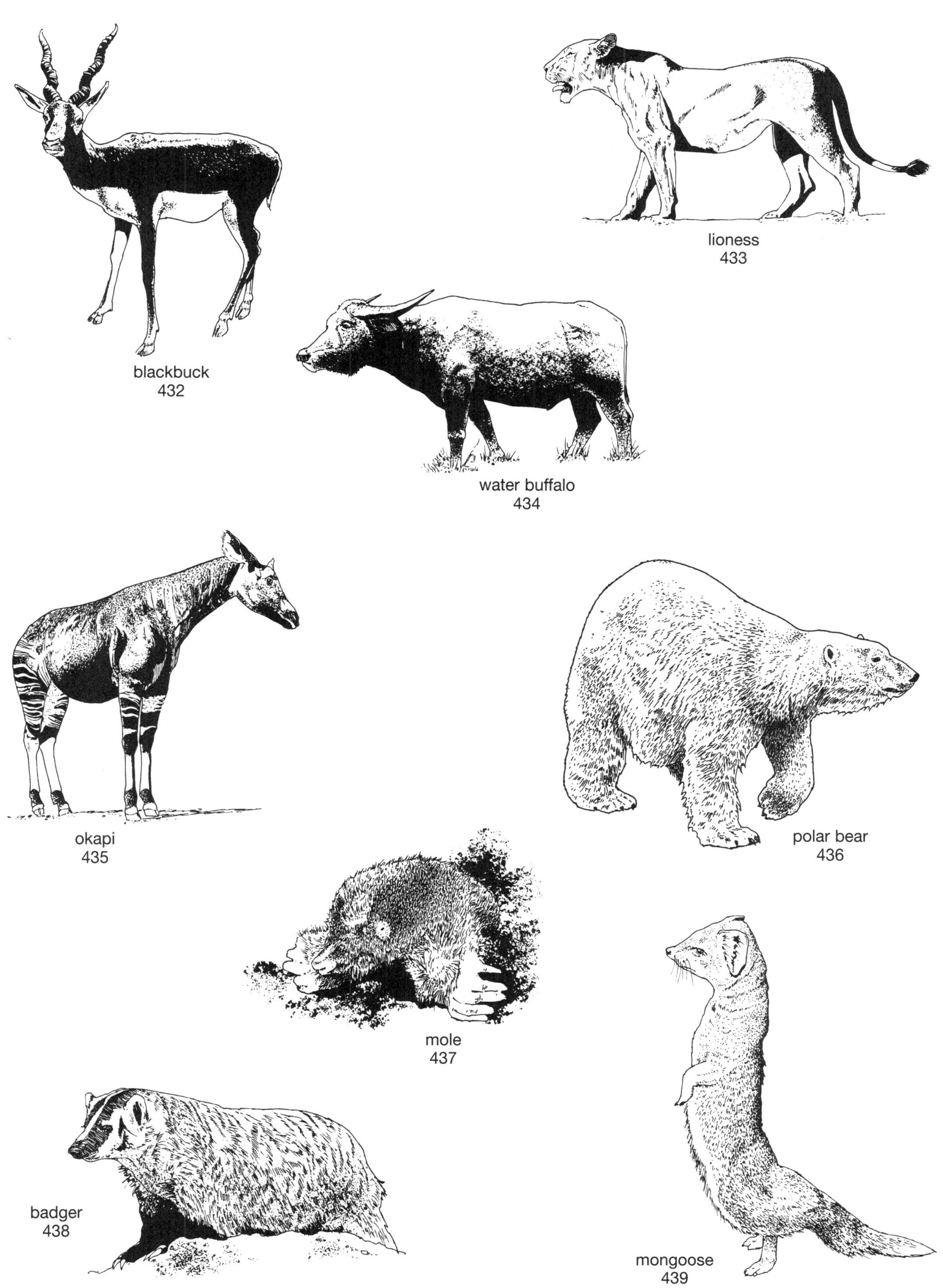
blackbuck
432
lioness
433
water buffalo
434
okapi
435
polar bear
436
mole
437
badger
438
mongoose
439

INDEX